Paranormal United States

Pursuit of the Paranormal

*To Patricia
Thank you for your support and hope you enjoy the book #stayweird*

Ash Ellis
Greg Thomlinson

Copyright © 2023 Pursuit of the Paranormal Podcast
All rights reserved.
ISBN: 9798853381018
Cover art by Greg Thomlinson

Foreword

As the host of the paranormal podcast Hillbilly Horror Stories, I try to consume as many books on the subject as possible. When I found out that fellow podcasters, Ash & Greg, were writing a book of 50 hauntings in the U.S., I couldn't wait to get my hands, or should I say my eyes, on it!

I was not disappointed. As an author myself, I know how much work goes into a project like this. Ash & Greg have definitely put their touch on these stories. As a regular listener to their podcast, Pursuit of the Paranormal, I can hear their voices as I read each story.

When I was asked to participate in writing this foreword, I was honored. Great job guys!

Jerry Paulley
Hillbilly Horror Stories

INTRO

Our 'Paranormal United States' series as part of the Pursuit of the Paranormal podcast came to be after we interviewed Jerry and Tracy Paulley from the super popular Hillbilly Horror Stories podcast (who have also very kindly agreed to write the foreword for this book)! Ash in particular was inspired by the sheer amount of episodes that the husband and wife team produce, and at the time only releasing one episode a week, became committed to producing more content.

This sparked the first 'series' to accompany our regular, weekly episodes. As both of us are fans of travel and the United States particularly, we decided to take a virtual tour of the country, visiting each state and taking in a specific creepy or paranormal story, or number of stories, from within that state.

What followed was a year-long journey, which soon proved to be popular with our listeners, and with ourselves as we discovered some very interesting, dark, and sometimes horrific, stories and tales from the other side of the pond.

This series was also the first time we recorded video to go with the audio podcast, which was a new thing for both of us, allowing us to give the viewer a visual of the places and buildings we visited along the way.

This book is intended to be a companion aide to the podcast series, often providing additional information to what we talk about in the original episodes. Although it can of course be read as a stand-alone book for anybody interested in spooky, and real, paranormal stories from across the United States of America. Each chapter is intended to be an introduction to that case or state, with further research or investigation encouraged!

In this book is a QR code which, once scanned, takes you to our YouTube channel where you can find all of the Paranormal United

States series as well as the rest of the Pursuit of the Paranormal podcast episodes, which cover a whole manner of topics from across the paranormal field including UFOs, cryptids, poltergeists, and of course hauntings, amongst much more.

None of this would be possible without the support of you, the listeners and fans, throughout the first years of our podcast. We can't express how much we appreciate every download, view, listen, comment, rating, feedback, and share, that you give us

THANK YOU!

Another first for us both, is actually writing a book! This has taken us well over 12 months from starting the first chapter to finally hitting publish but we are proud of what we have achieved both with the book and with our little podcast and we hope you enjoy reading it as much as we have enjoyed researching, writing, and recording, the...

Paranormal United States.

Cheers,
Ash & Greg
Pursuit of the Paranormal podcast

Paranormal United States

LISTEN NOW

Scan the QR code below to be taken to our Linktree page where you can listen to our podcast episodes, visit our website, read interviews and much more!

Alternatively search for **Pursuit of the Paranormal** or you can visit **www.linktree.com/pursuitoftheparanormal** or our website **www.pursuitoftheparanormal.co.uk**

Pursuit of the Paranormal

Chapter 1

ALABAMA

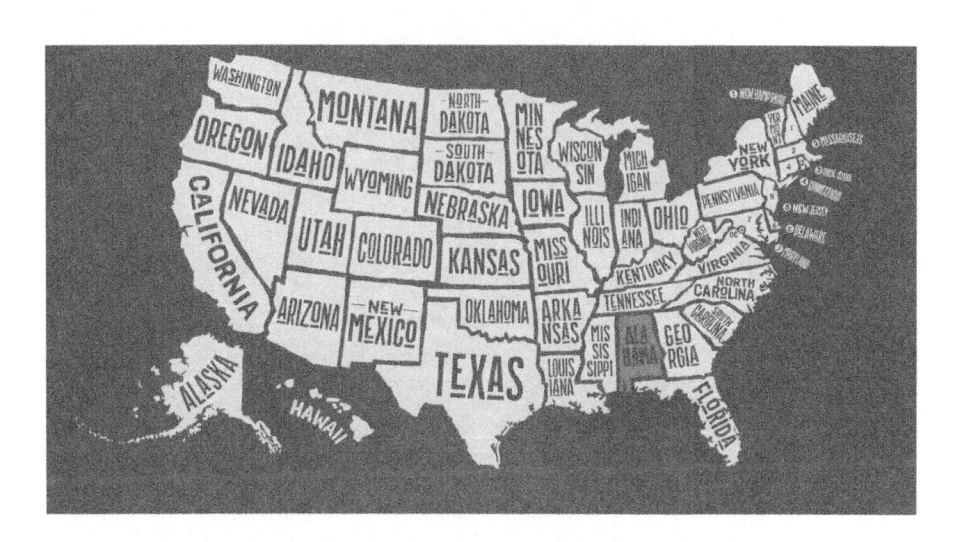

The Face in the Window

The Pickens County Courthouse in Carrollton, Alabama has a haunting tale associated with its history. Built in 1877, the courthouse was designed by the architect W.R. Gunn, and was built in the Greek Revival style. The courthouse has seen many historical events over the years, including the trials of several famous criminals, such as the trial of Robert Chambliss, who was convicted of the 1963 bombing of the 16th Street Baptist Church in Birmingham, Alabama.

Despite its historical significance, the courthouse is best known for one eerie phenomena — a ghostly face that appears in one of its garrett windows. This spectral image is believed to be that of Henry Wells, a freedman who met a tragic fate in 1878. The garret window, a skylight-type feature along the roof slope, holds the imprint of his fearful countenance.

Pickens Courthouse © Brian Collins www.atomicpix.com

Henry Wells was a former enslaved person who had been legally released from slavery. Considering the time period—late 19th century Alabama—social and racial tensions were high. Wells found himself in the spotlight when he was arrested in January 1878 under suspicion of burglary and arson, supposedly linked to the previous courthouse fire in 1876. He was taken to the sheriff's office located within the courthouse. Word of his arrest spread quickly, attracting a gathering crowd outside.

To protect Wells from the growing mob, he was confined to the high garret and instructed to remain silent. As the crowd continued to grow, their anger and desire for revenge focused on Wells. Overwhelmed by fear, Wells approached the garrett window and shouted down to the gathering, vehemently proclaiming his innocence. He warned them that if they killed him, he would haunt them for the rest of their lives.

In a twist of eerie coincidence, a lightning bolt struck nearby, briefly illuminating Wells' face contorted with fear for all to see. Undeterred by his plea and convinced of his guilt, the mob forcibly entered the courthouse, mercilessly taking Wells' life as he maintained his innocence.

The next morning, a member of the lynch mob passing by the courthouse was horrified to see Wells' face peering at him from the window, just as it had the previous night. He let out a scream, drawing the attention of others who also witnessed the ghostly image. Despite attempts to wash it away, the haunting face remains etched in the courthouse window, impervious to cleansing. Interestingly, severe storms have shattered every pane in the building, except the one that bears Wells' face.

Face In The Window © Brian Collins www.atomicpix.com

In the 1970s, the county erected a sign near the courthouse to commemorate the events that took place there. Binoculars were installed across the street, allowing curious individuals to get a closer look at the remaining trace of Henry Wells, the freedman caught in a tragic web of prejudice.

The lynching of Henry Wells was just one of fifteen such incidents that occurred in Pickens County between 1877 and 1917, making it one of the counties in Alabama with the highest number of recorded lynchings. This includes a notorious mass lynching of five African Americans in 1893.

The story of Henry Wells and the haunting face in the courthouse window serves as a chilling symbol of a dark era of racism that must never be forgotten or repeated. Numerous books have recounted variations of this tale, and it even inspired a play titled "The Face in the Courthouse Window," which debuted in April 2010 and is performed annually in the courthouse's courtroom.

Regardless of Wells' guilt or innocence, his presence lingers, silently watching over all who pass by the Pickens County Courthouse. The ghostly face in the window serves as a solemn reminder of the deep-seated racism that stained the region's history.

The Pickens County Courthouse is a building that is steeped in history and has a rich and mysterious past. While there is little concrete evidence to support the existence of the ghosts that are said to haunt the courthouse, the stories and legends surrounding the building continue to attract visitors and paranormal investigators from around the world.

Chapter 2

ALASKA

The Alaska Triangle

The Alaska Triangle is a vast, remote and rugged wilderness area in Alaska that has long been associated with unexplained disappearances of planes, boats, and people. The area covers around 200,000 square miles and is one of the most sparsely populated areas in the world, with only a few small towns and villages scattered throughout the region.

The terrain of the Alaska Triangle is challenging and includes rugged mountains, glaciers, dense forests, and icy waters. The extreme conditions in this area make it a dangerous place for those who venture into it. However, some of the people who have gone missing in the Alaska Triangle were experienced hikers, hunters, and pilots who were familiar with the area.

Pursuit of the Paranormal

The disappearances in the Alaska Triangle date back to the early 20th century, with reports of strange occurrences continuing to the present day. Despite the efforts of search and rescue teams, many of the missing people were never found, and their disappearances remain unexplained.

There have been many theories proposed to explain the strange occurrences in the Alaska Triangle. Some people believe that extraterrestrial activity is responsible for the disappearances. They point to reports of UFO sightings and alien abductions in the area as evidence of this theory.

Some of the most famous UFO sightings in the Alaska Triangle include the incident that occurred in November 1986 when a Japanese Airlines flight crew reported seeing a large, unidentified object flying near their plane. The incident, which has been dubbed the "Japan Airlines Flight 1628 incident," received international attention and sparked renewed interest in the possibility of extraterrestrial activity in the area.

The crew of the JAL Boeing 747 cargo freighter witnessed three unidentified objects after sunset while flying over eastern Alaska. The objects seemed to prefer the cover of darkness to their left, and to avoid the brighter skies to their right. At least the first two of the objects were observed by all three crew members: Captain Kenju Terauchi, an ex-fighter pilot with more than 10,000 hours flight experience, in the cockpit's left-hand seat; co-pilot Takanori

Every object possessed a square form, comprising two rectangular arrangements of luminous nozzles or thrusters, with a shadowy central division. Captain Terauchi's illustrations hinted at the possibility of the objects appearing cylindrical when observed from a different perspective, suggesting that the observed motion of the nozzles could be attributed to the rotation of these cylinders. Suddenly, the objects swiftly departed, heading towards a location below the eastern horizon.

It's also worth noting that many of the disappearances in the Alaska Triangle can be attributed to more mundane explanations, such as accidents, harsh weather conditions, and navigational errors. While these explanations may not be as exciting or mysterious as extraterrestrial activity, they are based on solid evidence and are more likely to be accurate.

The theory that natural phenomena could be responsible for the unexplained disappearances in the Alaska Triangle is one that has gained traction in recent years. One of the most popular theories is that strong geomagnetic forces in the area could be to blame. The region is located within the auroral oval, a zone around the magnetic North Pole where auroras are most common. This means that the area experiences strong magnetic activity, which could potentially interfere with navigational equipment, causing pilots and sailors to become disoriented and lose their bearings.

Matanuska Glacier, Alaska by Paxson Woelber licensed under CC BY 2.0

In addition to geomagnetic forces, some experts have suggested that unusual weather patterns could be responsible for the disappearances. The region is known for its extreme weather, with sudden storms and severe winds being a common occurrence.

Pursuit of the Paranormal

These weather patterns can be difficult to predict, and pilots and sailors may be caught off guard, leading to accidents or crashes.

There have been several cases where weather conditions were cited as a possible factor in the disappearances. For example, in 1972, a private plane carrying U.S. Congressman Hale Boggs and three other people disappeared in the area during a period of bad weather. Similarly, a U.S. Air Force C-124 Globemaster disappeared in 1950 which was flying through a storm when it vanished.

© 1972 New York Times Company

While natural phenomena could potentially explain some of the strange occurrences in the Alaska Triangle, it's important to note that these theories are still speculative and require further investigation. The rugged terrain and extreme weather conditions in the area can make it difficult to conduct thorough investigations, and many of the cases may remain unsolved.

The theory that the Alaska Triangle is a portal to another dimension is one of the more outlandish explanations for the unexplained disappearances in the area. According to this theory, there is a portal or doorway in the region that leads to another world or dimension. Some proponents of this theory have even suggested that the disappearances are a result of people accidentally wandering into this portal and becoming lost in another realm.

While this theory may sound far-fetched, it has gained some attention in popular culture and has been featured in several books and television shows. However, there is no scientific evidence to support the idea that the Alaska Triangle is a portal to another dimension. The idea of portals or gateways to other dimensions is a popular concept in science fiction and fantasy, but there is no scientific proof that such portals exist.

It's important to approach this theory with a critical eye and to consider the lack of evidence supporting it. While the Alaska Triangle is undoubtedly a mysterious and remote region with a long history of unexplained disappearances, there is no scientific basis for the idea that it is a portal to another dimension. It's more likely that the disappearances are the result of natural phenomena, human error, or other more plausible explanations.

The phenomenon of disappearances in the Alaskan Triangle is a complex and mysterious occurrence that continues to baffle researchers and authorities. While various theories attempt to provide explanations, the true reasons behind these disappearances remain elusive. Several factors contribute to the unique nature of the Alaskan Triangle and its heightened risk for individuals venturing into its vast and unforgiving wilderness.

Chapter 3

ARIZONA

The Yuma Territorial Prison

In the heart of Yuma County, stands the remnants of a bygone era - the Yuma Territorial Prison. Established in July 1876 and closed down in September 1909, this formidable institution once housed over 3,000 prisoners, predominantly males but also a significant number of females, serving time for crimes ranging from murder to polygamy. Perched atop a rugged hill, the prison overlooks the quaint town of Yuma, situated tantalisingly close to the California border.

Among the many spine-chilling tales associated with this historical site, one legend stands out. It revolves around the spirit of a little girl who met a tragic end in the nearby Colorado River while attempting to retrieve her fallen doll. This spectral presence is said to haunt the prison, manifesting as a mischievous and playful apparition, much like a child in life... and in death, it seems. She harbours a particular aversion to individuals clad in red, often pinching or poking them as they pass by. Children and adults alike have fallen victim to her pinches, seemingly chosen at random, earning her reputation as an entity with discerning dislikes!

The Yuma Territorial Prison holds a prominent place in the annals of paranormal activity, having attracted numerous television shows, including the popular series Ghost Adventures, which have filmed captivating investigations within its walls.

Yuma Territorial Prison State Park © Ken Lund under CC BY-SA 2.0

Many reports of supernatural encounters stem from a cell aptly nicknamed "the dark cell." This grim enclosure, devoid of any light, was utilised to punish inmates who violated prison regulations. Stripped down to their undergarments, the prisoners would be chained in place, with the sole source of illumination emanating from a minuscule ventilation shaft in the ceiling. As night fell, the ten-by-ten room plunged into absolute darkness. It is said that the guards would occasionally toss in scorpions, whimsically suggesting that the glowing creatures provided a modicum of light.

The psychological toll inflicted on those confined within these claustrophobic confines was so severe that some prisoners were subsequently sent to an insane asylum in Phoenix. Visitors often report feeling an overwhelming sense of unease within this particular area of the prison. Those who have braved the oppressive darkness describe an overwhelming suffocation and an inexplicable heaviness that discourages prolonged stays. A daring writer from a local magazine once planned to endure 48 hours in the cell, aiming to experience a fraction of the prisoners' torment. However, after enduring a mere 37 hours, she succumbed to an overwhelming sense of being watched, ultimately admitting defeat in the face of an unseen presence.

Yuma Territorial Prison State Park © Ken Lund under CC BY-SA 2.0

Further testimonies abound, recounting disembodied conversations echoing through empty rooms, fleeting glimpses of apparitions in the periphery of one's vision, a phantom woman serenading the visitors' area with her morning songs, and the spirits of deceased inmates manifesting along death row. Angry voices have even been heard, sternly warning unsuspecting visitors to evacuate the premises immediately!

Given the numerous fatalities that occurred within the prison's walls, including suicides and deaths resulting from a riot in 1887, it comes as no surprise that many souls appear to be trapped within its confines. Adding to the eerie atmosphere, the prison cemetery lies just a short distance downhill, perhaps contributing to the lingering spiritual energy.

Not limited to the cells and cell blocks, the paranormal activity extends its reach to the prison's museum, offices, and gift shop. Witnessed phenomena include objects moving of their own accord, lights flickering on and off inexplicably, and even coins spontaneously levitating from the cash register.

In 2019, the readers of USA Today voted the Yuma Territorial Prison as the best haunted destination in the entire country, solidifying its reputation as a hotspot for supernatural encounters.

Today, the prison stands as an integral part of the Yuma Territorial Prison State Park, inviting visitors to embark on a chilling journey through its storied past. The museum offers insight into the prison's history, while guided tours allow glimpses into the stark realities faced by its inhabitants.

The Yuma Territorial Prison remains a captivating testament to a tumultuous era in history, where the spirits of the past refuse to fade away. It serves as a chilling reminder of the harsh realities endured by those who were incarcerated within its walls. Whether you seek a brush with the supernatural or an appreciation for the resilience of the human spirit, a visit to this hauntingly atmospheric site promises an unforgettable experience.

Chapter 4

ARKANSAS

The Fouke Monster

In the dense forests and murky swamps of southeastern Arkansas, there lurks a creature that has fascinated and terrified locals for generations. Known as the Fouke Monster, this elusive cryptid is said to stand over seven feet tall, with a muscular build, scaly skin, and glowing red eyes. Some describe it as a type of Bigfoot, while others believe it to be a mutant alligator or some other type of reptilian monster.

The legend of the Fouke Monster dates back to the early 20th century, when sightings of a strange, bipedal creature were first reported in the area. Over the years, countless people have claimed to have seen the monster, often describing it as a terrifying and otherworldly creature that defies explanation.

One of the most famous sightings of the Fouke Monster occurred in the summer of 1971, when two teenage boys were out fishing on a remote swamp. As they paddled their boat along the murky waters, they suddenly spotted a large, scaly creature emerging from the nearby trees. The boys were terrified as the creature approached them, letting out a guttural roar that shook them to their core. After a few tense moments, the creature disappeared back into the forest, leaving the boys to wonder if what they had seen was real or just a figment of their imagination.

Since that fateful encounter, the legend of the Fouke Monster has only grown stronger, with more and more people coming forward with their own stories of sightings and encounters. Some have even claimed to have captured the creature on film or video, although none of these images have ever been verified as authentic.

Fouke Monster by Romana Klee is licensed under CC BY-SA 2.0

Despite the lack of concrete evidence, the legend of the Fouke Monster continues to captivate and terrify locals and visitors alike. Many people believe that the creature is an ancient, prehistoric beast that has somehow managed to survive into the modern era, while others speculate that it may be a new type of undiscovered species.

Pursuit of the Paranormal

Over the years, numerous expeditions and investigations have been launched in an attempt to uncover the truth behind the legend of the Fouke Monster. Researchers and cryptozoologists from around the world have travelled to Arkansas to study the creature, often braving the dense forests and treacherous swamps in search of evidence.

Despite their efforts, however, the Fouke Monster has remained elusive and mysterious, with no concrete evidence ever being found to prove its existence. Some researchers have theorised that the creature may be highly intelligent and able to evade capture, while others speculate that it may be a ghost or some other type of supernatural entity.

Despite the lack of evidence, the search for the Fouke Monster continues to this day, with new sightings and reports of encounters being reported every year. Some locals have even set up traps and cameras in an attempt to capture the creature on film, although so far none have been successful.

For many people, the search for the Fouke Monster is not just about proving its existence, but also about preserving the rich folklore and cultural heritage of the American South. The legend of the Fouke Monster has become an integral part of local history and tradition, with countless stories and songs being passed down from generation to generation.

Whether or not the Fouke Monster ever existed, its legacy lives on in the hearts and minds of the people of southeastern Arkansas. The creature has become an iconic symbol of the region, inspiring countless works of art, literature, and music.

In recent years, the legend of the Fouke has taken on a new life in popular culture, with references to the creature appearing in television shows, movies, and video games. It has become a part of the fabric of American folklore, alongside other famous monsters like Bigfoot and the Loch Ness Monster.

One notable example of the Fouke Monster's influence on popular culture is the 2013 horror film "The Legend of Boggy Creek," which takes place in Fouke, Arkansas, the alleged location of the creature's sightings. The film, which is loosely based on the legend of the Fouke Monster, follows a group of friends who encounter a terrifying creature while camping in the woods. The movie was a box office success, spawning a sequel and a remake, and cementing the Fouke Monster's place in the horror genre.

Beyond the realm of popular culture, the legend of the Fouke Monster has had a profound impact on the local community in Arkansas. The town of Fouke, which has embraced the creature as a part of its identity, hosts an annual "Boggy Creek Festival" to celebrate the legend and attract visitors to the area. The festival includes live music, food vendors, and a "Fouke Monster Calling Contest," in which participants attempt to recreate the creature's distinctive vocalisations.

But perhaps the most enduring legacy of the Fouke Monster is the sense of community and shared identity that it has inspired in the people of southeastern Arkansas. For generations, the legend of the creature has brought people together, forging connections between neighbours and strengthening the bonds of family and community.

Chapter 5

CALIFORNIA

The Haunted Playboy Mansion

The Playboy Mansion in Los Angeles, California, is known for its luxurious parties, lavish lifestyle, and celebrity residents. But what many people don't know is that the mansion is also rumoured to be haunted by the ghosts of its former inhabitants, including Playboy founder Hugh Hefner and his former girlfriends, who still linger in the halls, unable to leave their former home behind.

Despite these ghostly sightings, the mansion remains a popular destination for celebrities and tourists alike, drawn to its glamorous history and notorious reputation. But for those who believe in the supernatural, the mansion is more than just a playground for the rich and famous – it is a place where the dead still walk among the living.

Hugh Hefner, the founder of Playboy magazine and former resident of the Playboy Mansion, is a cultural icon who continues to influence popular culture long after his death. But for those who knew him, Hefner was more than just a media mogul – he was a charismatic and enigmatic figure, whose legacy extends far beyond the pages of his magazine.

In life, Hefner was known for his lavish parties, extravagant lifestyle, and endless parade of beautiful girlfriends. But despite his reputation as a playboy, Hefner was also a champion of free speech, civil rights, and sexual liberation, using his magazine as a platform to challenge conservative attitudes and promote progressive values.

The ghost of Hugh Hefner, dressed in his iconic silk pyjamas and smoking a cigar, has been seen multiple times, with some believing that he still roams the mansion, overseeing the parties and events that were such a big part of his life.

Regardless of the reasons behind his ghostly sightings, Hefner's legacy at the Playboy Mansion is undeniable. His influence on American culture and society continues to be felt, both in the pages of his magazine and in the hearts of those who remember him.

Hugh Hefner's Mansion © Carol M. Highsmith, Public domain

Pursuit of the Paranormal

One of the most famous incidents occurred in the late 1990s, when a group of Playboy Bunnies reported being terrorised by a ghostly presence in one of the mansion's bedrooms. The women claimed that they were unable to sleep due to the constant pounding and scratching on the walls and floor, and many reported feeling an icy coldness in the air.

Other incidents that have been reported at the Playboy Mansion include unexplained noises and footsteps, with the sounds of people walking around upstairs heard many times, despite the fact that the upper levels of the mansion are not in use.

Bridget Marquart, one of Hefner's ex-girlfriends and a familiar face in the mansion's heyday, recently shared her spine-chilling experience. While quietly watching television in one of the bedrooms, Marquart was startled by the sudden appearance of a woman standing in the doorway. The mysterious figure possessed long black hair, a ghostly pale complexion, and was clad in a white t-shirt. Despite emanating a positive energy, Bridget couldn't shake off the feeling of fear and unease. Although she couldn't pinpoint the identity of the spirit, she couldn't help but sense a vague familiarity, possibly having encountered the lady at a photo shoot many years ago. Marquart's encounter with the supernatural left her with a lingering sense of mystery and curiosity.

Holly Madison *(Inset: Holly Madison © Luke Ford, CC BY-SA 2.5)*, another former Playboy bunny and co-star of the reality TV show "The Girls Next Door," also had her own encounter with the unexplained at the Playboy Mansion. While in the mansion's basement gym, Madison witnessed the apparition of a woman. Startled, she observed as the ghostly figure emerged from the bathroom and glided across the room, eventually disappearing through a doorway. Unlike Marquart, Madison chose to dismiss the encounter, attributing it to a figment of her imagination. Despite her scepticism, it is worth noting that Madison did appear on an episode of the paranormal investigation series "Ghost Adventures," fueling further speculation about the mansion's supernatural aura.

The mansion's housekeeping staff, entrusted with maintaining the sprawling 2000 square metre property, have also voiced their concerns about eerie happenings within its walls. Numerous reports have surfaced of doors opening and closing on their own accord, accompanied by the inexplicable activation of video game machines in the games room. These unexplained incidents have left the staff perplexed, questioning the origin of these spectral phenomena.

With each account of these encounters, the haunted reputation of the Playboy Mansion grows, deepening the sense of intrigue surrounding its storied past. The mansion, once a symbol of hedonistic pleasure and opulent parties, now carries an air of mystery that extends beyond its lavish exterior. As the spectres of former employees and unknown entities continue to make their presence felt, it begs the question: is the Playboy Mansion really haunted, or are these occurrences mere coincidences and products of overactive imaginations?

However, for those who have experienced these strange occurrences firsthand, the reality of the Playboy Mansion's ghosts is difficult to deny. While the mansion may be known for its glamorous parties and celebrity guests, it is also a place with a rich and haunting history that continues to fascinate and intrigue people to this day.

Chapter 6

COLORADO

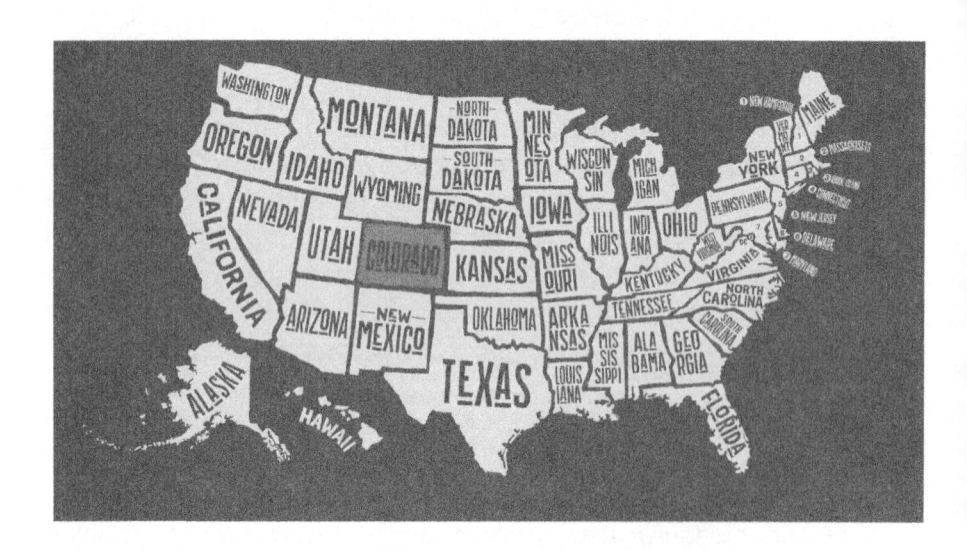

Denver International Airport

The Denver International Airport, located in Colorado, has long been a source of intrigue and controversy. From its mysterious artwork to its rumoured underground tunnels, the airport has captivated the imaginations of conspiracy theorists and curious travellers alike.

One of the most striking features of the airport is its unusual artwork. The most famous piece, a 32-foot-tall blue horse sculpture nicknamed "Blucifer," looms over the entrance to the airport. The statue's glowing red eyes and muscular physique have been the subject of many rumours and legends, with some claiming that it is a symbol of the Illuminati or a tribute to the Four Horsemen of the Apocalypse.

Other strange artworks found in the airport include murals depicting apocalyptic scenes and bizarre symbols, as well as a collection of gargoyles and other strange creatures. The artwork has sparked controversy and debate over its meaning and purpose, with some arguing that it is simply meant to be aesthetically pleasing, while others claim that it contains hidden messages and symbols.

Beyond the airport's artwork, there are also rumours of an extensive network of underground tunnels and bunkers located beneath the airport. Some speculate that these tunnels are part of a secret government facility, while others believe that they were constructed by the New World Order or some other mysterious organisation.

Although the airport has denied the existence of these tunnels, many visitors have reported strange occurrences and unexplained phenomena at the airport, experiences have only added to the airport's reputation as a strange and mysterious place.

Blucifer at the Denver International Airport © Mike Sinko by CC BY-SA 2.0

One of the most common reports from visitors is the sighting of mysterious figures lurking in the shadows. Some witnesses have claimed that these figures move silently through the airport's corridors and hidden areas, seeming to blend in with the shadows and remain unnoticed until they are directly encountered. Others have reported seeing the figures disappear suddenly, as if they were never really there.

Perhaps most unsettling of all are the reports of witnesses who claim that these figures have glowing eyes or other unusual features that suggest they are not of this world. Some have described the figures as having eyes that shine like red or green orbs, while others have claimed that they have seen figures with strange markings or symbols on their bodies.

While it is difficult to say for sure what these figures are or where they come from, some have speculated that they may be related to the airport's artwork or to the rumoured underground tunnels beneath the airport. Others believe that they may be spirits or other supernatural entities that are drawn to the airport's mysterious energy.

Gargoyle Statue © Bigmacthealmanac, CC BY-SA 4.0

Other visitors have reported hearing strange noises that seem to come from the walls or the floors of the airport. These noises are often described as being low, rumbling sounds or high-pitched whines, and they are said to be especially prominent in the more remote or less frequented areas of the airport.

Many visitors have also reported feeling a sense of unease or dread when passing through certain areas of the airport. Some have described feeling as though they are being watched or followed, while others have reported feeling a sudden drop in temperature or an inexplicable chill in the air.

While it is difficult to say what is causing these strange occurrences and feelings, some speculate that they may be related to the airport's artwork or the rumoured underground tunnels. Others believe that they may be the result of the airport's location on the high plains of Colorado, which has a reputation for being a hotspot for paranormal activity.

In addition to these strange phenomena, the airport has also been the site of numerous conspiracy theories and rumours over the years. Some have claimed that the airport was built on top of an ancient Native American burial ground, while others believe that it was designed to serve as a hub for a secret government operation or a meeting place for the Illuminati.

Despite the many rumours and legends surrounding the airport, however, there is little concrete evidence to support any of these claims. The airport has repeatedly denied any involvement in any secret government or Illuminati operations, and many of the alleged underground tunnels and bunkers have been debunked as simply being part of the airport's infrastructure.

Despite this, the strange artwork and eerie atmosphere of the Denver International Airport continue to fascinate and intrigue visitors from around the world. Whether it is simply a case of artistic expression or something more sinister, the airport's secrets and mysteries are sure to keep conspiracy theorists and curious travellers guessing for years to come.

Chapter 7

CONNECTICUT

The Norwich State Hospital

Norwich State Hospital, located in Preston, Connecticut, has a haunting past that dates back to its establishment in 1903. Originally known as the Norwich State Hospital for the Criminally Insane, this institution witnessed decades of turbulent history until its ultimate closure in 1996.

In its early years, Norwich State Hospital was a modest facility comprising a single building and housing only a handful of residents. However, as time progressed, the hospital experienced exponential growth, with additional structures being erected on its extensive grounds. At the height of its operation, it transformed into a self-sufficient village, boasting over 40 buildings and accommodating an astonishing population of more than three thousand residents.

While the hospital primarily served as a psychiatric institution, it also catered to individuals struggling with drug addiction, other dependencies, and even tuberculosis patients during a certain period. Unfortunately, like many institutions of its time, Norwich State Hospital lacked the knowledge and understanding necessary for appropriate mental health treatment. Tragically, the patients endured harrowing experiences as they became victims of barbaric methods employed in the name of medical care.

Norwich Hospital District Admin Building © CLK Hatcher, CC BY-SA 2.0

Mechanical restraints, electric shock treatments, and lobotomies were among the horrifying practices routinely inflicted upon the vulnerable patients. These techniques, now widely condemned, were not only ineffective but also deeply traumatising. Moreover, the patients suffered from a multitude of abuses, ranging from physical and sexual assault to being subjected to starvation, confinement, and even chilling experiments involving ice. Norwich State Hospital became a site of unspeakable suffering, where individuals seeking solace and recovery found themselves trapped in a nightmarish existence.

Regrettably, the horrors that took place within the hospital's walls did not end with these abhorrent practices. A lesser-known aspect of its dark history was the hospital's participation in eugenics programs aimed at controlling human procreation. Disturbingly, individuals deemed "mentally or psychologically ill" were forcibly sterilised, effectively preventing them from reproducing. Shockingly, nearly 600 people underwent this invasive procedure, the majority against their will, within the confines of Norwich State Hospital.

The hospital has long been rumoured to be a place of paranormal activity and unexplained phenomena. Over the years, many visitors to the abandoned hospital have reported strange occurrences, ghostly sightings, and other eerie experiences that have only added to the hospital's reputation as a place of mystery and intrigue.

One of the most common reports from visitors to the Norwich State Hospital is the sighting of ghostly figures moving through the hospital's abandoned corridors and rooms. These figures are often described as being shadowy and indistinct, with features that are difficult to make out in the dim light.

Many of these ghostly sightings are said to occur in the hospital's former patient wards, where visitors have reported feeling sudden drops in temperature or an inexplicable sense of unease or dread. Some have even reported hearing strange noises, such as the sound of footsteps echoing through the empty halls or the faint whispers of disembodied voices.

But it's not just the patients who are said to haunt the Norwich State Hospital. Some visitors have reported seeing ghostly images of the hospital's former staff, who are said to have been overworked and underpaid during their time at the hospital.

The ghost story of the nurse who committed suicide at the Norwich State Hospital is one of the most well-known tales associated with the hospital's paranormal activity. According to legend, the nurse was working in the hospital during the early 20th century, a time when conditions at the hospital were notoriously harsh and overcrowded.

As the story goes, the nurse became increasingly overwhelmed by the demands of her job, working long hours with little rest or support. Eventually, she was pushed to her breaking point and tragically took her own life on the hospital grounds.

Since then, visitors to the Norwich State Hospital have reported seeing the nurse's ghostly image walking the halls, still dressed in her nurse's uniform and carrying a clipboard. Some have reported feeling a sense of sadness or despair in her presence, as if they are witnessing the aftermath of her tragic decision.

The ghostly nurse is said to be most active in the hospital's former medical wing, where she is said to appear suddenly and then disappear just as quickly. Some visitors have even claimed to have heard the sound of her footsteps echoing through the empty corridors, as if she is still making her rounds through the hospital long after her death.

While some sceptics may dismiss the story of the nurse's ghost as nothing more than a legend, others believe that her spirit remains tied to the hospital, unable to move on from the tragic events that led to her untimely death.

Abandoned Theatre © Abandoned America www.abandonedamerica.us

Another common sighting at the Norwich State Hospital is that of a ghostly woman dressed in white. Some visitors have reported seeing her standing at the end of the hospital's long, dark hallways, beckoning them to follow her into the shadows.

But it's not just ghostly apparitions that visitors to the Norwich State Hospital have reported. Some have claimed to have experienced physical sensations or even to have been physically touched by unseen entities during their visits.

One visitor, for example, reported feeling a sudden pressure on her shoulders as if someone were pushing her from behind, while others have reported feeling a cold, clammy sensation on their skin as if they were being touched by a ghostly hand.

Some have even claimed to have seen objects move or levitate on their own, or to have heard strange, unexplained noises coming from empty rooms or corridors.

Of course, not everyone believes in the paranormal, and sceptics have been quick to dismiss the reports of ghostly sightings and other strange occurrences at the Norwich State Hospital as simply the product of overactive imaginations. But for those who have experienced these phenomena firsthand, the reality of the paranormal at the hospital is undeniable.

Whatever the truth behind the many ghost stories and legends associated with the Norwich State Hospital, one thing is clear: this abandoned institution remains a place of fascination and intrigue for those interested in the paranormal and the unexplained.

Chapter 8

DELAWARE

The Hauntings of Woodland

Nestled deep in the heart of Delaware lies the small town of Woodland, a place known for its scenic countryside and historic charm. But beyond its picturesque façade, Woodland has a reputation for being a hotspot of paranormal activity, with countless stories of ghosts, hauntings, and unexplained phenomena.

Woodland, a small community nestled along the banks of the Nanticoke River in Delaware, has gained notoriety for its spine-chilling tales of the paranormal. Among its many legends, one story stands out—the haunting of Maggie Bloxam and the infamous Maggie Bridge.

Dating back to the late 1800s, Maggie Bloxam met a tragic and gruesome end on the bridge that now bears her name. The circumstances surrounding her decapitation have left an indelible mark on the area, captivating the imaginations of locals and attracting paranormal enthusiasts from far and wide.

In the depths of the forest surrounding Maggie Bridge, eerie phenomena occur, giving credence to the belief that Maggie's spirit lingers on. Witnesses recount experiencing a heightened sense of presence during full moon nights, accompanied by strange and inexplicable noises emanating from the woods. Perhaps the most unsettling sight is that of Maggie's apparition, forever condemned to roam the area, carrying her severed head. Even electronic devices seem to fall victim to the paranormal influence, malfunctioning inexplicably within the forest's ethereal confines.

Maggie's Bridge © Chesapeake Ghosts https://chesapeakeghosts.com

Some sceptics dismiss Maggie's haunting as mere folklore, attributing it to the fertile imaginations of those fascinated by the supernatural. However, there is more to Maggie's story than meets the eye. Historical records confirm that Maggie Bloxam was, in fact, a real person who once walked among the living. Her grave lies nearby, further lending credence to the belief that her restless spirit still wanders the land she once called home.

But Maggie's presence is not the only spectral enigma haunting Woodland. Another ghostly apparition has been sighted near the river, believed to be a member of a notorious family whose dark legacy adds another layer of intrigue to the town's paranormal tapestry.

Woodland's haunting history extends beyond individual tragedies. In 1903, a devastating smallpox outbreak swept through the area, leading to the quarantine of the Woodland ferry region. Cut off from the outside world, residents faced a harrowing ordeal, deprived of essential supplies and medical aid. Many succumbed to the disease, their bodies interred in a mass grave without proper markings, forever leaving a lingering aura of sorrow and despair. It is within the confines of this unmarked resting place that paranormal activity is said to occur, as restless spirits seek solace and redemption.

Compounding the mysteries of Woodland is the lack of comprehensive census data, leaving the town's population shrouded in uncertainty. However, its tumultuous history paints a vivid picture of decapitations, murders, and pandemics that have shaped the community. Tales of desperation and resilience intertwine, with the town's pleas for quarantine during the smallpox outbreak echoing through the ages—a plea that ultimately led to mixed outcomes and haunting repercussions.

One prominent landmark in Woodland that holds its own share of eerie secrets is the Cannonball House. Constructed in 1765, this historic property has served various purposes throughout its existence, from housing a restaurant to operating as a laundromat and private residence for pilots. Presently under the ownership of the Lewes Historical Society, the house bears the name derived from a cannonball that struck its foundation in 1813—an event that has left an indelible mark on its haunted reputation.

"Cannonball House" by jjmusgrove is licensed under CC BY 2.0

Woodland's haunted legacy extends beyond the confines of the Cannonball House. Multiple other properties in the area have reported strange occurrences and unexplained phenomena. Rivs Halt House, in particular, has garnered attention for its otherworldly happenings, while even the founder of Delmarva Historic Haunts, an organisation specialising in paranormal investigations, claims to have experienced inexplicable touches during his explorations of the area.

Delaware itself has a long and storied history intertwined with folklore and strange happenings. The smallpox outbreak that ravaged Woodland serves as a stark reminder of the fragility of life and the lingering impact of such tragic events. Although confined to a specific area, the outbreak's repercussions reverberated throughout the state, leaving behind an atmosphere tinged with sorrow and an increased susceptibility to paranormal occurrences.

Delaware's rich historical tapestry, coupled with its proximity to the unknown and unexplained, makes it a fertile ground for those seeking encounters with the supernatural. From ghostly apparitions to inexplicable lights reminiscent of UFOs, the state has become a haven for paranormal enthusiasts and researchers alike.

Woodland, Delaware, stands as a testament to the enduring allure of the paranormal. Its haunted tales and tragedies continue to captivate the minds and hearts of those drawn to the mysteries that lie beyond the veil of our reality. Whether it be the restless spirit of Maggie Bloxam or the lingering spectres of the smallpox outbreak, the stories embedded within the town's fabric serve as reminders of the delicate balance between the seen and the unseen, the known and the unknowable.

As the nights grow darker and the whispers of the past grow louder, Woodland remains an enigmatic destination for those seeking a brush with the supernatural. Whether driven by a desire to unravel the truth behind the legends or simply to experience a thrill beyond the ordinary, the haunted tales of Woodland, Delaware, continue to beckon, inviting us to explore the depths of the unknown and venture into the realms where reality and the paranormal intertwine.

Chapter 9

FLORIDA

The Skunk Ape

The Skunk Ape is a legendary creature that is said to inhabit the swamps and forests of Florida, primarily in the southern part of the state. Described as smaller than its Bigfoot counterparts, the Skunk Ape exhibits distinct features, such as a white stripe adorning its head, reminiscent of a skunk. However, its most notorious characteristic is its pungent odour. Witnesses have reported an overwhelming stench emanating from the creature, earning it the name "Skunk Ape," a foul smell believed to be produced by the creature's fur.

Since the 1950s, reports of man-sized monkey sightings in Florida have surged, contributing to the Skunk Ape lore,with The Bigfoot Field Researchers Organization holding hundreds of alleged reports, beginning in 1955 into the present day.

Interestingly, the existence of similar creatures predates these accounts, with an early newspaper report dating back to 1818. Witnesses often describe the Skunk Ape as non-confrontational, preferring to flee when encountered. This behaviour aligns with the flight reflex commonly observed in cryptids and indicates their instinctual drive to avoid harm.

In 1929, a remarkable event unfolded near the Perky Bat Tower in Florida Keys, which had been constructed not long ago. According to eyewitness accounts, a creature with a resemblance to an ape was drawn to the site. Intriguingly, as the bat tower was being examined shortly after the bats had been introduced, this peculiar being rattled the structure, causing the bats to scatter in fear, and swiftly vanished into the depths of the nearby woods.

Is this a Skunk Ape captured on video? © Dave Shealy

In the 1970s there was a sighting by two Palm Beach County sheriffs, Marvin Lewis and Ernie Milner, who were on a routine patrol when they spotted a large, bipedal creature that they described as resembling an ape or a gorilla. The creature was said to be about 7 feet tall, covered in dark hair, and emitting a strong, foul odour.

The sheriffs claimed that they shot at the creature and then followed footprints but were only able to recover a small amount of hair snagged on a barbed wire fence line that had been pushed down.

The incident gained national attention when it was reported in newspapers and on television news programs. The Palm Beach County Sheriff's Office conducted an investigation into the sighting, but was unable to provide any conclusive evidence to support or refute the claims made by the two officers.

Critics of the sighting argue that it may have been a misidentification of a known animal, such as a bear or an orangutan that had escaped from captivity. However, believers in the Skunk Ape legend point to the officers' credibility as law enforcement officials as evidence that their encounter was legitimate.

In 1977, Florida counties considered passing a bill to protect humanoid animals, including the Skunk Ape. Although the bill did not pass, it revealed a collective concern to safeguard these enigmatic creatures from harm. On a lighter note, lawmakers also attempted to pass joke laws related to the Skunk Ape. However, their efforts proved unsuccessful, showcasing the delicate balance between preserving folklore and enacting legislation.

In July 1997, Vince Doer, the chief of the Occupy Fire Control District, and Jan Brock, a real estate agent, independently witnessed the creature while driving through the Everglades. Delaware's fire chief even managed to capture a photograph of the elusive creature before it vanished into the forest. Within two weeks, over fifty people reported alleged sightings of a hairy creature within the Big Cypress National Preserve.

In the year 2000, the Sarasota County Sheriff's Office found themselves in possession of two intriguing photographs sent anonymously. These pictures depicted a remarkable creature resembling a large, hairy, and ape-like being. The sender, an elderly woman, claimed to have captured the images after stumbling upon the creature pilfering apples from her back porch near I-75. Fearing for her family's safety, she hastily snapped the photographs, believing the creature to be an escaped orangutan.

The authenticity of these photographs, widely known as the "Myakka Skunk ape," continues to be a subject of intense debate, further fueling the controversy surrounding them. One argument against their legitimacy points out the striking resemblance the subject bears to a Bigfoot statue famously exhibited at a Ripley's Believe It or Not! Museum.

Inset: "Skunk Ape Cast Expedition Bigfoot The Sasquatch Museum Blue Ridge Georgia" by amanderson2 is licensed under CC BY-SA 2.0

Remarkably, sightings of similar creatures persist to this day, as evidenced by reports from a significant number of counties in Florida. Since 2010 alone, forty-eight out of sixty-seven counties in the state have documented encounters with these elusive beings.

The Skunk Ape continues to captivate the imagination of those fascinated by the paranormal and cryptozoology. With its skunk-like appearance, pungent odour, and sightings by high-ranking officials, this elusive creature remains an enduring mystery. While sceptics may dismiss the Skunk Ape as a product of folklore and misidentifications, the reports and cultural impact surrounding it cannot be easily dismissed. As Florida's very own version of Bigfoot, the Skunk Ape adds a touch of the supernatural to the state's already diverse and captivating landscape.

Chapter 10

GEORGIA

The Ghosts and Monsters of Lake Lanier

Georgia is a state known for its captivating landscapes and intriguing tales, but none are quite as chilling as the sinister stories and urban legends that surround its largest lake, Lake Lanier. Nestled amidst the breathtaking beauty of Georgia's countryside, this seemingly serene body of water hides a dark history filled with mysterious deaths and ghostly sightings.

Originally intended as a reservoir to meet the water needs of Georgia and neighbouring states, Lake Lanier has become shrouded in a veil of tragedy and unexplained phenomena. The unregulated water flow, while initially serving its purpose, has caused death and destruction, leaving behind a trail of sorrow and uncertainty.

Since its creation in 1956, nearly 700 people have died at Lake Lanier, with some of the more deadly years claiming over 30 lives. Accidents and unexplained deaths continue to occur, creating a sense of unease for visitors and locals. In one of the most tragic incidents, on Christmas Day in 1964, the lake claimed the lives of several individuals, leading to hundreds of people gathering on its shores to mourn.

Scientists and researchers have offered various explanations for the dangerous and unpredictable nature of the lake. One theory is that the flooding of the Oscarville community during the creation of the lake caused disruptions in ancestral burial grounds, leading to the curse of Lake Lanier. Another explanation is that the lake is simply not safe, with hidden currents and dangerous debris making it prone to accidents.

Lake Lanier July 2018 © Thomson200, CC0 Public domain

Despite these explanations, many people believe that there is something more sinister at work. The area around Lake Lanier is steeped in legends and folklore, with tales of ghosts and monsters intertwined with the lake's history of tragic accidents and deaths. Many visitors have reported sightings and experiences that cannot be explained by science, with some claiming to have encountered the ghost of Allatoona, the woman who drowned her children in the lake and now haunts the area looking for them.

The Lady of the Lake is a legendary ghost that is said to haunt the lake, traced back to a tragic incident that occurred in 1958. Two women named Delia Parker Young and Susie Roberts were driving across the lake bridge when their car plunged into the water, leading to their demise. Susie was wearing a blue dress at the time of their accident, which has become a key part of the legend.

The legend of the Lady of the Lake began to spread after the discovery of Delia Parker Young's body near the bridge about a year after the accident. As locals near Dawsonville started to believe that the body might have been Susie Roberts, the ghost stories started to emerge. Some reports suggest that Susie's ghost appears in a blue dress, wandering near the bridge at night, lost and restless.

There have been many reported sightings of the Lady of the Lake over the years. Witnesses have described a female figure wearing a blue dress, or a woman who seems to be walking on water. Others claim to have seen the figure of a woman swimming beneath the surface of the lake, as if reliving her final moments. Although the phenomenon remains a mystery, believers see it as a tragic reminder of the dangers of Lake Lanier.

Urban legends about peculiar creatures dwelling within Lake Lanier have also emerged over time. One such tale revolves around a woman whose newborn baby exhibited the features of a catfish. Dubbed "Fish Head," the baby had small eyes, a lipless mouth, and pale grey skin. As he grew up, the child was ridiculed and made fun of so much that he shrank from society. Two men decided to capture the boy so they set out in a boat and approached where the boy was said to live, in woods near the lake. A splash was heard and a few minutes later, they were gone. Nothing was ever found except their boat with claw marks on the side as if some animal had grabbed the side and turned the boat over.

Reports of a mysterious raft equipped with a lantern and ridden by a shadowy figure have also left witnesses awestruck. The ghostly vessel materialises out of thin air, defying the laws of reality. In one account, two bewildered fishermen witnessed the raft's appearance, only for the shadowy figure to disembark and swim towards them. As a spotlight was shone upon the lantern, it inexplicably extinguished.

Beneath the picturesque surface of Georgia's largest lake lies a tapestry of tragedy, ghostly apparitions, and unexplained phenomena. As visitors and locals alike explore its waters, they are met with a potent mix of awe and trepidation, knowing that Lake Lanier's mysteries may never truly be unravelled.

Chapter 11

HAWAII

The Spirits of Morgan's Corner and Old Pali Road

While Hawaii may be renowned for its stunning beaches and vibrant culture, it also holds the distinction of being one of the most haunted states in the United States. Despite its relatively small size, the islands are home to a high number of reported paranormal phenomena.

Nestled along the eerie expanse of the old Pali Road, Morgan's Corner has acquired a notorious reputation among paranormal investigators. Just a stone's throw away from the Pali lookout, a majestic cliff overlooking Oahu, this corner possesses a history steeped in darkness. The cliff itself witnessed a grim event in 1795 when over 400 warriors were forced off its precipice, leaving behind an energy that still lingers to this day. Visitors and locals alike have reported hearing haunting howls and cries echoing through the night, believed to be the tormented spirits of the fallen warriors.

However, it was in 1948 that Morgan's Corner etched its name into the annals of macabre history. Two escaped convicts perpetrated a heinous murder in this desolate location, forever cementing its association with fear and dread. The victim, Widow Theresa Wilder, met a gruesome fate during a brutal home invasion. Bound, beaten, and gagged in her own bed, she became a tragic victim of an unspeakable act of violence. The perpetrators were eventually captured and sentenced to death, but their punishment was later commuted, leaving justice unfulfilled.

Pali Road somewhere between 1883 and 1905
© Gabriel Bertram Bellinghausen, Public domain

It is said that the ghostly presence of Widow Theresa Wilder still roams the grounds of Morgan's Corner, her anguished screams reverberating through the night. Witnesses have recounted bone-chilling encounters with the half-faced phantom, believed to be

Pursuit of the Paranormal

the restless spirit of a teenage girl who suffered a grim fate. The decomposed body of this unfortunate victim was discovered in a ravine, her face gruesomely disfigured, likely the result of animal predation. The murder remains unsolved to this day, with a police officer as the prime suspect, but no conclusive evidence leading to a conviction

Adding to the enigma surrounding Morgan's Corner, an open investigation into the alleged rape and murder committed by a sheriff continues to baffle authorities. Mishandling of the initial postmortem examination led to a dearth of evidence, hindering progress in solving this heinous crime. Despite multiple reopenings of the case and meticulous reexaminations of the body, no one has been held accountable for the horrific act. The grieving parents of the victim passed away without ever knowing the truth. Speculations arise regarding a potential connection between this case and reported apparitions in the vicinity, further fueling the air of mystery surrounding Morgan's Corner.

In addition to the haunted history of Morgan's Corner, the adjacent Old Pali Road harbours its own paranormal tales. According to the legends, the Pali Highway was constructed on top of a sacred site where ancient Hawaiian warriors were buried. During the road's construction, workers accidentally disturbed human remains, which is said to have triggered a curse upon the road. This curse, it is believed, has led to a series of tragic incidents over the years, including fatal accidents and suicides. Additionally, there are claims of ghostly apparitions being seen along the road and eerie voices heard in the surrounding woods.

The haunting stories of Hawaii would be incomplete without delving into its rich folklore. One particularly captivating legend revolves around the tumultuous relationship between Pele, the goddess of fire, and Kamapuawa, a human demigod embodying both man and pig. The tale warns against disregarding the boundaries set between these two entities. It is believed that transporting pork over the Old Pali Road transgresses these sacred boundaries, allowing Kamapuawa's power to infiltrate Pele's domain. Those who dare defy this prohibition risk encountering Pele's wrath, resulting in car troubles and the eerie appearance and growth of a mysterious dog-like entity, which grows in size until the pork is either discarded or an unconventional remedy is employed - urinating on the driver's side tyre.

Pali Lookout © InSapphoWeTrust CC BY-SA 2.0

For those who are interested in the supernatural and enjoy a thrill, visiting these sites during daylight hours can offer a unique and potentially eerie experience. However, it is essential to approach these locations with respect and caution, as some locals strongly believe that the spirits of the deceased should not be disturbed. Trespassing or attempting to disturb the area is highly discouraged and disrespectful.

The Pali Highway legends not only showcase the rich cultural heritage of Hawaii but also demonstrate the power of storytelling in shaping our perception of a place. Whether or not one believes in the supernatural, these tales contribute to the sense of mystery and allure that surrounds the Pali Highway, making it an intriguing destination for those fascinated by both history and the unknown.

Chapter 12

IDAHO

The Haunted Pocatello High School

Pocatello High School, nestled in the southeastern region of Idaho, has gained a notorious reputation as one of the most haunted high schools in the state and potentially the entire country. The town of Pocatello itself is steeped in a rich history, giving rise to its eerie tales and paranormal legends. In 2014, the school's haunting stories captured national attention when security footage of unexplained phenomena during winter break went viral

Uncovering the origins of Pocatello High School's ghostly tales leads us to a heart-wrenching story. Originally constructed in 1892, the school experienced a devastating fire in 1914. Legend has it that a young girl, embroiled in a tragic suicide pact with her friend, met her demise within the school's walls. The spirit of this tormented soul is said to linger, forever haunting Pocatello High School.

At the heart of the school's supernatural reputation lies a perplexing encounter captured on video. At precisely 1:33 on the footage, a shadowy figure emerges, moving in and out of the bathroom and along the dimly lit hallways. This enigmatic sighting has sparked great enthusiasm among both ghost hunters and local news stations, with many speculating that the figure could be a ghost. The presence of this mysterious apparition further amplifies the school's haunted allure.

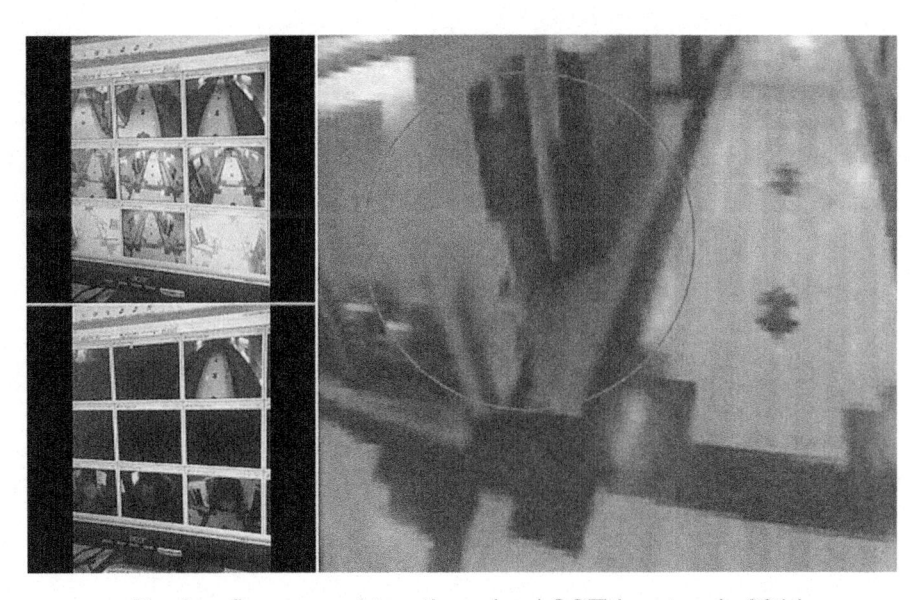

Shadow figure caught on the school CCTV system in 2014

Records reveal six confirmed deaths that occurred within the school's premises, providing a chilling backdrop to the countless reports of ghostly encounters. Students have shared eerie experiences such as flickering lights and mysteriously closing doors, fostering a pervasive atmosphere of otherworldly presence.

Beyond the collective school-wide hauntings, specific areas within Pocatello High School harbour intriguing ghost stories. A janitor, working in the salvaged section of the building, once stumbled upon a young boy whose ethereal presence defied explanation. Additionally, the school's library holds a chilling tale of a librarian who met her tragic end by hanging herself from a chandelier. Many claim to have witnessed her ghostly apparition gazing through the windows, perpetuating the librarian's rumoured haunting.

Pocatello High © Beantwo, CC BY-SA 3.0

One of the most intriguing and commonly reported occurrences at Pocatello High School is the presence of phantom footsteps that echo through empty hallways. Numerous students and staff members have attested to hearing these eerie sounds when no one else is present. The unexplained nature of these footsteps has sparked speculation and curiosity about the possible presence of spirits within the school.

These phantom footsteps have been reported in various parts of the school, occurring during both day and night. Some witnesses describe them as light and hesitant, like the steps of a curious child, while others insist they resemble the heavy and deliberate tread of an adult. The enigmatic nature of these footfalls, combined with their ability to manifest in different areas of the school, adds to the mystery surrounding their origin.

One explanation offered by believers in the supernatural is that these phantom footsteps are the residual energy of former students or staff members who once walked the halls of Pocatello High School. According to this theory, the imprints of their presence become imprinted in the environment, resulting in the auditory manifestation of their footsteps long after their physical existence has ceased.

Sceptics, on the other hand, often attribute these mysterious sounds to natural causes. They propose that old buildings like Pocatello High School tend to creak and settle over time, resulting in sounds that can be mistaken for footsteps. Additionally, temperature changes, air currents, and other environmental factors can create acoustic illusions, leading to the perception of footsteps where none exist.

However, what sets apart the experiences at Pocatello High School is the consistency of these reports and the credibility of the witnesses. Many of those who have encountered the phantom footsteps are reputable individuals, including teachers, administrators, and long-time residents of the community. Their sincerity and the similarity of their accounts lend weight to the possibility that there may be something beyond the realm of conventional explanation occurring within the school's walls.

Adding another layer to the enigma, there are rumours of a secret underground tunnel beneath Pocatello High School. According to local legends, this hidden passageway served various purposes throughout the school's history, from providing escape routes during emergencies to being used by clandestine groups, joining up with one of the many other underground secret passageways below the city of Pocatello and the wider Idaho area.

Despite the eerie tales, Pocatello High School holds a special place in the hearts of its students and staff members. Many individuals view the hauntings as an integral part of the school's unique history, embracing the ghostly reputation as a source of pride. Rather than being frightened or deterred by the supernatural stories, they celebrate the school's mysterious past, further enhancing its charm and appeal.

The school's status as one of the most haunted high schools in Idaho and possibly the entire country is unquestionably well-deserved. With the mysterious shadowy figure caught on video, the tragic tale of the suicide pact, and the various ghostly encounters reported throughout the school's history, the paranormal realm seems to have entwined itself deeply within its walls. As long as the whispers of Pocatello's haunted past endure, the curious and the brave will continue to seek out the truth behind the chilling legends that surround this infamous high school.

Chapter 13

ILLINOIS

The Hauntings of Alton

Alton, a quaint town nestled on the banks of the majestic Mississippi River, has gained quite a reputation as the most haunted small town in America. Steeped in rich history and adorned with intriguing tales and legends, Alton is a place where the veil between the living and the spirit world seems particularly thin.

Dating back to 1869, the McPike House stands as a relic of the past and a hotspot for ghostly encounters. It is believed that the spirits of its original owners, Eleanor and Henry McPike, still roam the corridors of this historic mansion. Visitors to the house often report witnessing orbs floating in the air, inexplicable lights flickering in the darkness, and hearing eerie noises echoing through the rooms. The fact that the McPike House is situated on Native American land further fuels the paranormal occurrences, lending an air of mystique to this already haunted dwelling. Some even speculate a possible connection to an underground railway stop, adding another layer of intrigue to the haunted narrative. The area surrounding the house, with its abandoned buildings and an atmosphere of forgotten times, only heightens the supernatural aura that permeates the McPike House.

Another intriguing location in Alton is the first Unitarian Church, a place with a captivating history of fire and resilience. Originally constructed in 1830, the church suffered the misfortune of burning down in 1850, only to be reconstructed and struck by fire once more in 1901. Despite these tragic incidents, the church was rebuilt in 1905 and has since stood as a testament to the human spirit's unwavering determination. However, the paranormal phenomena associated with the church go beyond the mere tragedies of fire. In 1934, the church's reverend fell ill and experienced inexplicable symptoms, which only added to the reports of supernatural occurrences within its walls.

Alton Military Prison. Unknown author Public domain

Moving on to the infamous Alton prison, Illinois' first state penitentiary which opened in 1833 for just 27 years before the remaining prisoners were moved to another facility in 1860. In 1862 after some improvements were made, the prison was reopened as the Alton Federal Military Prison, and housed over fourteen thousand Confederate soldiers during the Civil War. With over 1,400 prisoners succumbing to the harsh conditions, including a devastating smallpox outbreak, the prison became a grim reminder of the toll taken by the war. The bodies of the deceased were buried on a nearby island aptly named Smallpox Island, all of which now lies underwater.

One cannot explore the supernatural side of Alton without mentioning the Mineral Springs Hotel, with its dark and chilling past. Even the construction of the five-storey hotel in 1913 had dark beginnings, with stone from the Alton Military Prison used to build the hotel's foundations! Known for its ghost sightings and tragic deaths, the hotel has since become a hub for paranormal enthusiasts.

One of the prominent spirits said to haunt the premises is that of a 17-year-old boy, seen wearing a brown suit and often spotted near the pool area. Legend has it that he met his untimely demise by drowning. Another ghostly presence is that of a young girl named Cassandra, who is said to have drowned during a birthday celebration held at the hotel, her child spirit continuing to play with her beloved marbles even in the afterlife.

Mineral Springs Hotel, Alton IL © Great Rivers & Routes Tourism
www.riversandroutes.com

Near the former pool area, you may encounter a male spirit known as George, who is believed to have died by drowning in the 1920's. Is this the same man who appears as an apparition in the old bottling room? These are just a few of the many alleged ghostly inhabitants of the haunted Mineral Springs Hotel.

As we delve deeper into the paranormal investigations conducted in this small town, we discover a rich tapestry of ghost tours and explorations that have further unravelled Alton's mysteries. Pink orbs floating in the air and electronic voice phenomena (EVP) recordings have become synonymous with the supernatural activity experienced in Alton, lending credibility to the claims of a highly active spirit realm.

With a population of approximately 25,000, Alton might seem like an unlikely candidate for a hotbed of paranormal activity. However, the age and historical significance of its buildings and walls serve as conduits for the ethereal energy that permeates this town. Alton stands as a testament to the enduring allure of the paranormal, where the line between the tangible and the intangible blurs, and the realms of the living and the dead intertwine in a captivating dance.

Chapter 14

INDIANA

A Whirlwind Tour of Haunted Locations

Welcome to Indiana, a state brimming with rich history, vibrant culture, and spine-tingling ghost stories. Embark on a whirlwind tour of the haunted locations scattered across this captivating state, spanning from bustling cities to tranquil countryside. Prepare yourself for a journey that delves into the past and explores the mysteries that linger in the present.

Our first destination on this thrilling expedition brings us to the heart of Indianapolis, the vibrant capital city of Indiana. Steeped in history and known for its bustling energy, Indianapolis sets the stage for a captivating encounter with the paranormal at the renowned Hannah House.

The Hannah House stands as a silent witness to the harrowing era of the Underground Railroad, a network of secret routes and safe houses that aided enslaved individuals in their quest for freedom.

Pursuit of the Paranormal

Originally built in 1858 by Alexander Hannah, this beautiful Italianate-style mansion played a crucial role in sheltering fugitive slaves on their arduous journey to liberty. The house provided a sanctuary for those seeking refuge from the horrors of slavery, becoming a beacon of hope in a time of darkness.

However, the Hannah House's noble purpose does not overshadow the tragic stories of its former residents. Ghost enthusiasts are drawn to the Hannah House, yearning to witness firsthand the ethereal remnants of the past that still linger within its walls. From disembodied voices and unexplained footsteps to doors mysteriously opening and closing, the paranormal activity reported here is enough to send shivers down anyone's spine. Visitors have even claimed to catch glimpses of ghostly apparitions, as if the spirits of those who sought refuge within the house continue to inhabit its spaces.

The Hannah House serves not only as a fascinating historical landmark but also as a portal into a haunting and tragic chapter of America's past. It offers a unique opportunity to connect with the spirits of the Underground Railroad, to honour their struggles and sacrifices, and to bear witness to the resilience of the human spirit.

Continuing our captivating journey through Indianapolis, we find ourselves drawn to the enigmatic Crown Hill Cemetery, one of the largest cemeteries in the United States sprawling across a vast expanse of land, its rolling hills and towering trees casting an otherworldly shadow over the landscape. It is a place steeped in history, with its first burial dating back to 1864. The cemetery serves as the final resting place for numerous notable individuals, including politicians, artists, and even infamous outlaws, adding to its allure and mystique.

One of the most well-known legends associated with Crown Hill Cemetery revolves around the tombstone of famous bank robber John Dillinger. According to local lore, Dillinger's ghost is said to wander the grounds, forever bound to the place of his burial. Some visitors claim to have witnessed his apparition, dressed in his iconic pinstripe suit, as he roams the cemetery in eternal restlessness.

Crown Hill Cemetery Gateway Arches © Tom Woodward, CC BY-SA 2.0

But Dillinger's spectre is not the only one rumoured to haunt this sacred ground. Countless stories abound of shadowy figures that dart between the gravestones, ethereal voices that echo through the night, and inexplicable cold spots that send a chill down one's spine. Those who are sensitive to the supernatural often describe an indescribable energy permeating the air, as if the spirits of the departed are still present, lingering between this world and the next.

Nestled in the heart of Indiana lies the French Lick Springs Hotel, a world-class resort renowned for its opulence and fascinating history. This majestic establishment boasts spas, golf courses, fine dining, and even a casino. Throughout its illustrious past, it has welcomed distinguished guests such as Al Capone, Bob Hope, Franklin D. Roosevelt, and Duke Ellington. However, beyond the glamour lies an eerie presence. Many believe that the spirit of its former owner, Thomas Taggart, still roams the premises, making his presence known through mysterious scents and apparitions. Guests and staff have reported chilling encounters, from cold spots and phantom

Pursuit of the Paranormal

footsteps to laughter emanating from empty rooms and inexplicable phone calls.

If you find yourself becoming thirsty, then tucked away in Indianapolis is the Slippery Noodle Inn, Indiana's oldest drinking establishment, which has a long history riddled with legends of hauntings. Dating back to 1850, this iconic venue is said to be frequented by spirits of deceased prostitutes, and in 1953, the establishment abruptly closed its doors after a murder, leaving behind a lingering sense of unrest. Guests, particularly men who venture upstairs, have reported encounters with the ghosts of the past, doors mysteriously opening and closing whilst apparitions and unseen forces unsettle the staff, further cementing the Noodle's reputation as a paranormal hotspot.

Slippery Noodle Inn © Sarah Stierch CC BY 4.0

Meanwhile, in Mitchell, Whispers Estate awaits those seeking an encounter with the paranormal. This 3,700 square foot Victorian home is shrouded in stories of spectral phenomena. Visitors have reported nightmares, unexplained tremors, and the sensation of an otherworldly presence sitting on their chest. The property's infamous whispering voices and paranormal encounters have attracted both casual tourists and dedicated ghost hunters alike.

Indiana, with its captivating blend of history and supernatural lore, offers an enticing array of haunted destinations. Whether you find yourself exploring the bustling cities or the tranquil countryside, be prepared for encounters that defy explanation and stories that will send shivers down your spine. Embark on this journey, embrace the unknown, and immerse yourself in the hauntingly beautiful world of Indiana's ghostly tales.

Chapter 15

IOWA

The Villisca Axe Murders

On June 10, 1912, the quaint town of Villisca, Iowa would forever be scarred by a series of gruesome events that transpired within the Moore family home. This chapter delves deep into the bone-chilling details and haunting aftermath of Villisca Axe Murders, a perplexing unsolved crime that has left investigators and the community perplexed for over a century.

As the sun slipped beneath the horizon and darkness settled upon the streets, an unknown malevolent presence emerged, choosing this fateful night to unleash its malevolence. Slipping through an unlocked door, the intruder took advantage of the household's slumber, completely ignoring the unsuspecting girls downstairs. Guided solely by the feeble light of a lamp and possessing an eerie familiarity with the layout of the house, the intruder stealthily ascended the stairs, wrapping the atmosphere in an ominous shroud.

With each room encountered, the assailant ruthlessly committed unspeakable violence, staining the walls with innocent blood. The Moore family and their guests became helpless pawns in a macabre theatre orchestrated by this enigmatic figure. And just as swiftly as the intruder appeared, they vanished into the night, leaving behind a bone-chilling tableau of carnage and despair.

Inside the Moore residence, a scene of unspeakable horror awaited those who stumbled upon it. All eight victims, including children as young as six, had been bludgeoned beyond recognition, their bodies left to bear the grotesque marks of a merciless killer. But the horror did not conclude with the loss of lives - it was only the beginning.

Law enforcement found themselves perplexed, left with shockingly few leads to unravel this brutal event. Various suspects were named throughout the investigation, but no definitive connections could be established, and the true identity of the Villisca Axe Murderer eluded capture.

As the investigation widened its scope, disturbingly similar crimes with uncanny resemblances to the Villisca Axe Murders unfolded in different parts of the country. Yet, despite these eerie parallels, no concrete connections could be established. With time, the case grew cold, and the once-infamous house was abandoned, its doors locked to preserve the echoes of terror within its walls.

However, the legacy of the Villisca Axe Murders refused to fade into obscurity. The house became a magnet for seekers of the supernatural, as rumours of paranormal activities swirled around it. Visitors reported hearing whispers and blood-curdling screams, while the sound of an axe swinging through the air sent shivers down the spines of all who dared venture inside. Shadowy figures seemed to materialise, lurking in the corners of the house, perpetuating the feeling that the Moore family's souls were trapped within its confines. Some individuals claim to have seen a man with an axe roaming the hallways.

Pursuit of the Paranormal

LAST VICTIMS OF MAD MURDERER OF WEST

J. W. Moore, wife and 3 of 4 children who were murdered in bed at Villisca, Ia. Star shows room in which Misses Stillinger, visiting Moores, were killed.

During the last two years, a madman murderer has killed four whole families in the West. In each case he used an axe. The murders have been at Colorado Springs, Ellsworth, Kan., Guilford, Mo., and Villisca, Ia. The last, that of the Moores at Villisca, occurred this week. The slayer shows a terrible ingenuity in making good his escape. Villisca police arrested Sam Moyer, relative of Moore family. Produced alibi. Released.

—o—o—

Irishman: "Give me three cigars."
Shopman: "Strong or mild?"
Irishman: "Give me the strong ones. The weak ones break in my pocket!"

Chicago News © The Day Book, Public domain

Mediums and psychics were drawn to the Villisca Murder House like moths to a flame, eager to communicate with the restless spirits of the victims. Their encounters fueled the growing intrigue, as the spirits conveyed their anguish and confusion from beyond the grave, unable to find peace. Even the courageous souls who spent a night within its walls faced inexplicable phenomena - apparitions of the murdered family members, eerie drops in temperature, objects moving without explanation, and unexplained electrical disturbances.

Today, the Villisca Axe Murder House stands as a chilling testimony to the unfathomable depths of the human soul and of unspeakable evil. Boarded up and abandoned, it serves as a stark reminder of the devastation that can be wrought upon innocent lives within the sanctity of their own home.

Over a century has passed since that fateful night in 1912, but the mystery remains unsolved. The small town of Villisca, once a close-knit community, was forever changed by the grisly events that unfolded within the Moore family home. Suspicion ran rampant, and neighbours began to view each other with fear and doubt, wondering if the friendly faces next door concealed secrets as sinister as those witnessed that night.

Josiah B. and Sara Moore House © Jason McLaren CC BY-SA 4.0

In today's modern era, the fascination with the Villisca Axe Murders endures. True crime enthusiasts still pour over the evidence and theories, trying to unlock the truth that has remained hidden for over a century. The case has found its way into books, documentaries, and podcasts, captivating audiences with its chilling blend of horror and mystery.

In 2014, a paranormal investigator at the house was rushed to hospital after being found with a self-inflicted stab wound to his chest. Robert Steven Laursen Jr from Wisconsin, was alone in one of the bedrooms whilst the rest of his group were outside, when he called one of them who found him and called the emergency services. There has been no explanation for this action with police ruling out any foul play.

The Villisca Murder House, now open as a museum, continues to draw visitors from around the world. Guided tours allow people to step back in time, to experience the eerie ambiance that lingers within its walls. Some witnesses experience unexplained phenomena during their visit, feeling the weight of the past and hearing echoes of the victims' anguished voices.

The Villisca Axe Murders remain a chilling chapter in American crime history, a series of events that continue to perplex and disturb. As long as the mystery remains unsolved, the Villisca Murder House will stand as a haunting testament to the relentless search for answers and the reminder of evil that can strike at any moment.

Chapter 16

KANSAS

The Hauntings of Sallie House

Nestled in Atchison, Kansas, at 508 N. Second Street, lies the legendary Sallie House—a dwelling steeped in ominous history and renowned as the epitome of haunted homes in America. Its mystique has both captivated and terrorised individuals around the world.

Constructed in the 1800s, this mid-century residence stands as a testament to the passage of time. Boasting three bedrooms and two bathrooms within its modest 1,200 square feet, the house was originally erected for Michael Finney and his family, who would intermittently inhabit the premises for several generations until 1947.

Tragically, the Finney family bore witness to the natural passing of four of its members within the walls of this dwelling, each succumbing to the relentless grip of mortality at different points in time. However, it is a single fateful incident that would etch the Sallie House into the annals of paranormal folklore, forever intertwining its legacy with the spectral realm.

Dr Charles Finney and his family resided upstairs while the front of the house was transformed into office space and examination rooms. It was on a fateful day that a desperate mother arrived, cradling her 6-year-old daughter, Sallie, her face contorted in agony. Gripped by excruciating abdominal pain, the child's life hung in the balance.

Swiftly diagnosing appendicitis and aware that immediate surgery was imperative, the doctor wasted no time. Unbeknownst to Sallie, her tiny frame convulsed with fear as the physician commenced the operation before the anaesthesia could take full effect. Trapped in a waking nightmare, Sallie's cries abruptly ceased, replaced by a pallid stillness. She drew her last breath on the operating table, her final memories a harrowing testament to the torment she believed had befallen her.

Sallie House © Visit Atchison, https://visitatchison.com

With the passage of time, the Sallie House exchanged hands, each owner adding their own chapter to its dark narrative. However, it was Tony and Debra Pickman, a young couple who acquired the property in the 1990s, that would solidify its notoriety. From the moment they stepped foot within its walls, they found themselves immersed in a disconcerting world of unexplainable occurrences, veering toward the malevolent.

Initially, the manifestations were subtle - lights flickering, inexplicable cold spots, toys engaging in unaided play, and perplexing changes in animal behaviour. However, with the arrival of their son, the intensity heightened

The lights in his nursery would inexplicably remain on throughout the night, and strange moulds would form on various household items. A pivotal moment arrived when the couple discovered their meticulously arranged nursery stuffed animals scattered on the floor, arranged in a haunting circle. Terrified, they sought refuge elsewhere, only to be confronted by an inexplicable burning sensation on Tony Pickman's back. Three enigmatic scratches marred his skin, a portent of the escalating malevolence that plagued their lives.

Desperate for answers, the Pickmans enlisted the aid of psychic medium Barbara Connor. Her visit to the Sallie House aimed to unravel the enigma that held the family captive. Connor posited that a spectral presence, that of Sallie, sought attention from the inhabitants, her ethereal existence a haunting plea for recognition. Attempting to embrace the spirit as a spectral daughter, the couple's efforts proved futile. The malevolent force continued its onslaught, culminating in a horrifying incident during their child's birthday party — a doll inexplicably consumed by flames. In a final act of defiance against perpetual terror, the Pickmans abandoned the house, leaving behind their nightmarish ordeal

A litany of paranormal phenomena has been attributed to the Sallie House, propelling it into the media spotlight for over two decades. Its spectral tales have been immortalised in many popular TV shows as well as in the book 'The Sallie House Haunting: A True Story' authored by Debra Pickman and was also the subject of a Showtime movie called 'Haunted Heartland.'

The reported hauntings within the Sallie House encompass a vast spectrum, encompassing the eerie and the inexplicable. Witnesses have testified to witnessing full-bodied apparitions, including the poignant presence of a young girl. Mysteriously, candles have been known to ignite without cause, leaving behind burnt fingerprints as cryptic evidence. Objects levitate through the air, disembodied voices echo in the night, and the walls reverberate with scratching and the disconcerting sounds of furniture being rearranged. Reports of physical attacks and instances of possession further blur the line between the supernatural and the tangible.

As the legend of the Sallie House continues to grow, so does the fascination with the paranormal. Kansas has become a destination for those seeking answers to the unexplained, and the Sallie House remains at the forefront of this enigmatic landscape. Whether it is truly a haunted dwelling or a complex web of psychological and environmental factors, one thing is certain: the Sallie House will continue to bewitch and bewilder all who dare to venture within its haunted halls.

Chapter 17

KENTUCKY

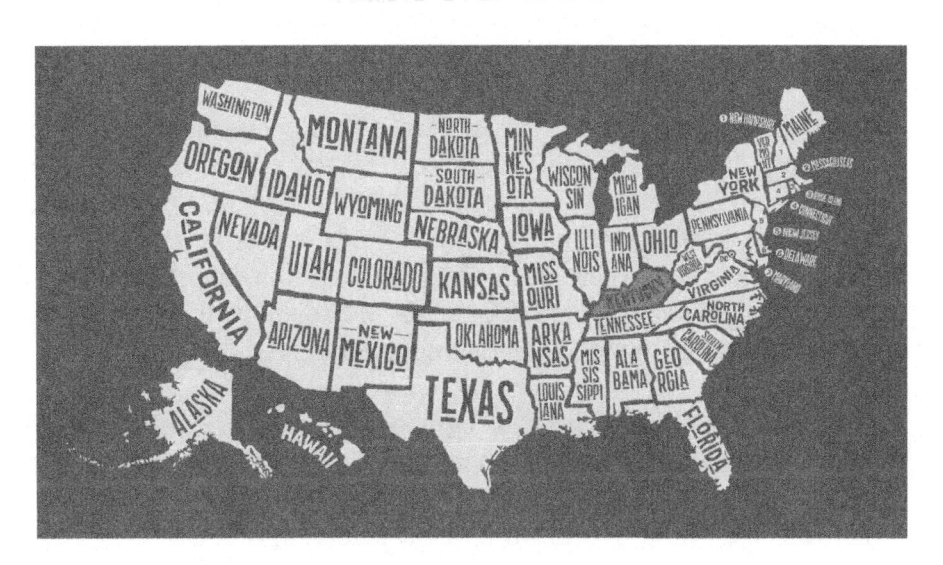

The Kelly-Hopkinsville Goblins

In the annals of UFO encounters, few incidents have captured the imagination quite like the Kelly–Hopkinsville encounter of 1955. Nestled in the picturesque landscapes of Christian County, Kentucky, the rural towns of Kelly and Hopkinsville became the backdrop for an extraordinary event that would leave an indelible mark on the realm of ufology. This claimed close encounter with extraterrestrial beings continues to be hailed by UFOlogists as one of the most compelling and extensively documented cases in the annals of UFO history. However, sceptics dismiss the reports as the result of misinterpretations and the effects of heightened excitement. The incident has even found its place as an academic example of pseudoscience, aiding in the cultivation of critical thinking among students.

On the fateful evening of August 21, 1955, the tranquillity of the region was shattered when five adults and seven children sought refuge at the Hopkinsville police station. Their harrowing tale spoke of otherworldly creatures descending upon their farmhouse, launching an assault that had been repelled with gunfire over a relentless span of nearly four hours. Elmer Sutton and Billy Ray Taylor, two of the adults, recounted their encounters with a group of short, dark figures—twelve to fifteen in number—who persistently appeared at doorways and peered through windows.

Alarmed by the potential escalation of violence, local authorities, including city police, state troopers, deputy sheriffs, and military police from nearby Fort Campbell, swiftly responded to the Sutton farmhouse in Kelly. A thorough search of the premises revealed no trace of the alleged intruders, save for the aftermath of gunfire and the perforated window and door screens, testimony to the desperate resistance put up by the besieged occupants.

The farmhouse was inhabited by a cluster of individuals, including Glennie Lankford and her children Lonnie, Charlton, and Mary, Elmer "Lucky" Sutton and his wife Vera, John Charley "J.C." Sutton and his wife Alene, Alene's brother O.P. Baker, and Billy Ray Taylor and his wife June. The Taylors, along with "Lucky" and Vera Sutton, were transient carnival workers who happened to be visiting the farmhouse. Curiously, the following day, neighbours informed authorities that the families had abruptly vacated the premises, their departure prompted by the alleged return of the enigmatic creatures at approximately 3:30 in the morning.

News of the otherworldly encounter swiftly spread, capturing the attention of local and national media. Initial reports did not mention the iconic "little green men," with the colour being added to subsequent newspaper articles. Descriptions of the alleged creatures varied, ranging from two to four feet in height, accompanied by details such as large pointed ears, claw-like hands, glowing yellow eyes, and spindly legs — an amalgamation of accounts that permeated various media outlets.

For psychologists Rodney Schmaltz and Scott Lilienfeld, this alleged incident serves as a case study in pseudoscience, enabling students to hone their critical thinking skills and differentiate between truth and fiction. Schmaltz suggests that the sightings could plausibly be attributed to the presence of Great Horned Owls, further speculating that the witnesses may have been influenced by intoxication during the purported "alien attack."

Supporting this viewpoint, author Brian Dunning draws striking parallels between the reported creatures and the aggressive behaviour of local Great Horned Owls, which stand at a height of approximately two-thirds of a metre.

UFOlogist Jerome Clark, however, portrays a different picture, recounting that the alleged creatures seemingly floated among the trees while bullets striking them produced a metallic sound akin to hitting a bucket. Clark also describes an enigmatic luminous patch along a fence, resulting from the shooting of one of the beings, and a mysterious green light emanating from the nearby woods—yet these phenomena align with the presence of foxfire, a bioluminescent fungus found on decaying wood.

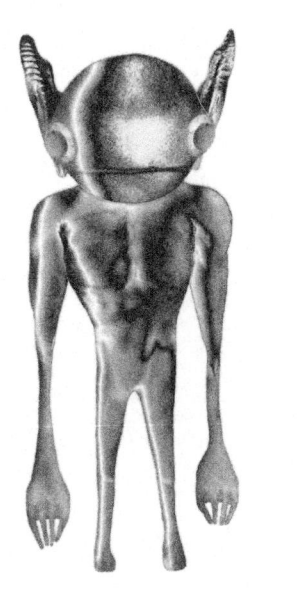

Hopkinsville goblin by Tim Bertelink is licensed under CC BY-SA 4.0

While investigations by the police, Air Force officers from Fort Campbell, and civilian UFOlogists failed to uncover evidence of a hoax, Brian Dunning questions the popular notion that Air Force investigators arrived at the scene the following day, noting the absence of corroborating evidence. Dunning further highlights that the military police accompanying the officers hailed from an Army base rather than an Air Force installation.

The alleged creatures, often likened to gremlins, have since been dubbed the "Hopkinsville Goblins" in popular culture. Their protracted visitation and the considerable number of witnesses involved have rendered this case notable. Project Blue Book, the U.S. Air Force's official study of UFOs dismissed the incident as a hoax without any further commentary.

The Kelly–Hopkinsville encounter remains an enigma, caught between belief and scepticism, inviting speculation and debate. Whether it was an extraordinary visitation from extraterrestrial beings or a series of misidentifications fueled by excitement, one thing is certain: the allure of this peculiar encounter endures, captivating both ufologists and sceptics alike.

Chapter 18

LOUISIANA

The Haunted LaLaurie Mansion

Marie Delphine Macarty was born on March 19, 1787, in New Orleans, which was then known as Spanish Louisiana. Both of her parents held prominent positions within the European Creole community of the town.

At the age of 13, Delphine entered into matrimony with Don Ramón de Lopez y Angulo, a distinguished officer in the Spanish royal hierarchy. Tragically, during their journey to Madrid, Don Ramón passed away suddenly in Havana, leaving Delphine, who was also pregnant at the time, in a state of mourning.

In June 1808, Delphine found love once again and married Jean Blanque, an esteemed figure in the fields of banking, commerce, law, and legislation. However, sorrow struck Delphine's life yet again when Blanque passed away in 1816, leaving her a widow.

Determined to move forward, Delphine embarked on her third marriage, this time to Leonard Louis Nicolas LaLaurie, a physician. On June 25, 1825, they commissioned the construction of a magnificent two-story mansion at 1140 Royal Street. The grand residence included slave quarters that were attached to the main building.

Delphine LaLaurie © Unknown author, Public domain

Accounts of Delphine LaLaurie's treatment of her slaves between 1831 and 1834 vary, with some conflicting reports and mixed testimonies. Shocking tales emerged, including that of a young girl who, driven to desperation by Lalaurie's cruelty, leaped to her death after enduring brutal whippings. Lantern-lit burials were conducted in the mansion's backyard, ensuring the secrets remained hidden. While there were public rumours about her mistreatment of slaves on her property, a local lawyer dispatched to investigate found no evidence of wrongdoing or mistreatment during his visit.

However, the shocking truth came to light on April 10, 1834, when a devastating fire engulfed Delphine LaLaurie's Royal Street mansion. As rescuers rushed to extinguish the flames and save the inhabitants, they made a horrifying discovery in the attic. Bound slaves, who had been held captive, were found showing visible signs of cruel and violent abuse that had occurred over an extended period.

The exact details of the abuse suffered by these enslaved individuals were appalling. Eyewitness accounts from that fateful day and subsequent investigations revealed the slaves with their limbs apparently stretched and torn, displaying the gruesome aftermath of unimaginable torment. The victims spoke of enduring long periods of imprisonment and enduring severe physical and emotional abuse at the hands of Delphine LaLaurie.

The public outcry was immediate and intense. News of the abused slaves and the cruel conditions they endured quickly spread throughout New Orleans, prompting outrage among the city's residents. The discovery of such atrocities shook the community to its core, challenging the prevailing societal norms and shining a light on the inhumanity of slavery.

LaLaurie Mansion © APK, CC BY-SA 4.0

Pursuit of the Paranormal

The Lalaurie Mansion's dark history did not end with the fire. The Lalaurie family, shunned by society, fled to Paris, where Madame Lalaurie spent the rest of her days carrying the weight of her crimes. Meanwhile, the mansion took on various roles throughout the years. It served as a girls' school, a shelter for the homeless, a private residence, and even housed a bustling pub at one point. Each new chapter added to the layers of paranormal energy that enveloped the building.

Renowned actor Nicholas Cage once owned the haunted mansion, intending to use it as inspiration for a horror novel. However, the eerie presence of spirits, including apparitions of slaves, proved too much for him. Madame Lorry, the former mistress of the house, has reportedly been banished from the mansion but continues to haunt a nearby cemetery where she once worshipped.

Delphine LaLaurie died in December 1849, in Paris, France, with the exact date of her death remaining disputed.

The mansion traditionally held to be LaLaurie's is a landmark in the French Quarter, known as the "LaLaurie Mansion." However, her original house was burned by the mob, and the current mansion was rebuilt after her departure from New Orleans.

The Lalaurie Mansion stands as a chilling testament to the darkest aspects of Louisiana's haunted history. Madame Lalaurie's vile actions and the suffering endured by her slaves have forever stained the walls of this once magnificent home. Despite renovations and changes of ownership, the mansion's ominous presence persists, earning its reputation as one of the most haunted mansions in New Orleans. As visitors pass by, they are reminded of the haunting past and the importance of never forgetting the horrors that occurred within those walls—a nod to the tragic history of New Orleans itself.

Chapter 19

MAINE

The Legends and Hauntings of Bucksport

Maine, known for its picturesque landscapes and serene coastal towns, harbours a sinister secret within its borders. Tucked away amidst the natural beauty lies Bucksport, a small town that has gained notoriety for its spine-chilling paranormal activity. From eerie apparitions to mysterious disappearances, Bucksport has become the focal point of supernatural intrigue, earning its reputation as the most haunted town in Maine.

Bucksport's haunting legacy is intertwined with the chilling tale of Buck's Tomb, a place that has earned Bucksport the reputation of being Maine's most haunted town. The legend revolves around Colonel Jonathan Buck, the town's esteemed founder. His tragic tale unfolds with a love affair gone awry, leading to the expulsion of his lover, who later gives birth to their son. In a heartless act, Buck refuses to aid her in caring for the child and falsely accuses her of witchcraft. She meets a tragic end, consumed by flames. However, her son, driven by love, retrieves her severed leg and enshrines it as a poignant memorial. Strangely, even Colonel Buck's final resting place, a grandiose tomb, bears an indelible stain resembling a spectral leg. Despite multiple attempts to remove the apparition by replacing the stone, the leg-shaped imprint remains — an enduring testament to a haunting past.

Buck's Tomb (with leg imprint still visible) © DrStew82, CC BY-SA 4.0

Delving deeper into Bucksport's haunted history, we explore the mysterious "Cemetery for the Lost Red Paint People." These enigmatic indigenous people inhabited Maine long before the arrival of other settlers, leaving behind traces of their existence. In Bucksport, remnants of their presence can be found scattered throughout the town, with the current cemetery on McDonald's Street acting as a poignant reminder. It is said that these sacred grounds were interwoven with the land, their resting place marked by red okra. Even today, the town pays homage to this ancient tradition, with many older homes adorned in red, reminiscent of the red paint used by the native tribes.

One such site steeped in mystery is the Robinson House. This historic structure, also known as Jed Paltry's Senior Centre, has stood since the 1780s, bearing witness to a multitude of significant events that have shaped the town of Bucksport. However, beneath its quaint exterior lies a dark history of criminal activity and unexplained hauntings. During the era of prohibition, the house harboured a secret, operating as a clandestine tavern and serving as a hub for smuggling illicit goods.

Ghost hunters have ventured into its shadowy corridors, only to confirm the supernatural presence that lingers within. Poltergeists manifest their mischievous presence, delighting in moving objects and creating an eerie atmosphere. There are also whispers of ethereal ladies of the night, apparitions that embody the secrets and scandals that once unfolded within the house's walls. These spectral women, forever trapped between the realms of the living and the dead.

Bucksport from the Penobscot River © Leonard G.CC SA 1.0

While the haunted locations paint a chilling portrait of Bucksport, it is the burial ground that adds an element of intrigue to the town's supernatural reputation. Rumours swirl about the disappearance of Sarah Ware, a notable resident who vanished in 1898, her headless body later discovered under baffling circumstances. The burial ground itself holds a connection to the strange happenings, reminiscent of the paranormal phenomena depicted in the movie Poltergeist. So profound is its reputation that an insurance company once refused to pay out, citing the burial ground as an act of God. Speculation runs rampant regarding the secrets entombed within, with some suggesting that Sarah Ware's body or head may lie within its hallowed ground.

Bucksport's eerie atmosphere extends beyond the burial ground, permeating other unusual locations within the town. Silver Lake, a man-made reservoir, hides a haunting secret beneath its tranquil surface. Local legends whisper of bodies and tombstones from untransferred graves resting in its depths, contributing to the restless energy that envelops the area. Similarly, the Trim family murder of 1876 casts a lingering shadow over Bucksport. The remains of the Trim family's granddaughter were never found, leaving an unsettling void in the tragic narrative. Both Silver Lake and the street named after the Trim family serve as reminders of the spectral presence that looms over the town.

Bucksport's history is not solely marked by tales of hauntings and enigmatic disappearances. The Penobscot Expedition, a significant event in Maine's past, unfolded along the town's nearby river. The battle, which occurred during the Revolutionary War, resulted in the largest loss of lives in the United States Navy until the bombing of Pearl Harbor. The river itself played a pivotal role in the region's lumber industry, claiming the lives of workers who laboured along its banks. Ghostly apparitions of these individuals have been sighted, eternally bound to the water's edge. The river's proximity to Prospect, home of the infamous haunted Fort Knox, further deepens the region's aura of otherworldly encounters.

Fort Knox, a formidable structure that never witnessed battle during the Revolutionary War, holds its own paranormal secrets. Despite a lack of notable deaths within its walls, sightings of spectral soldiers persist, evoking a chilling presence that transcends time. As a sentinel guarding the small town of Bucksport, Fort Knox has become synonymous with eerie sightings and unexplained phenomena, adding to the town's reputation as a hotbed of supernatural occurrences.

Chapter 20

MARYLAND

Chesapeake and Ohio Canal Hauntings

The Chesapeake and Ohio Canal, affectionately known as the C&O Canal, served as a vital link between Washington DC and Cumberland. Stretching nearly 185 miles, this historical waterway operated from 1831 to 1924, primarily transporting coal from the Allegheny Mountains. Today, the canal stands as a national historical park, brimming with fascinating stories of ghostly encounters and haunted locations. In this article, we will delve into the chilling legends that surround the C&O Canal and its captivating history.

Beyond its role in transportation and commerce, the C&O Canal has become synonymous with eerie tales and spectral sightings. Numerous haunted spots dot its length, adding an air of mystery to its already intriguing past. One such location is Haunted House Bend, near Edwards Ferry, where the echoes of a turbulent Civil War period still resonate. The canal's proximity to the Battle of Ball's

Bluff has led to stories of fallen soldiers finding their eternal rest within its murky waters.

Many unfortunate souls met their demise in the canal, their bodies floating downstream to Washington. It is said that the lingering spirits of these fallen soldiers haunt the area. Over the years, boatmen on the canal reported spine-chilling screams and moans emanating from the haunted house bend. Some even refused to moor their boats there at night, opting to continue their journeys unsettled by the otherworldly phenomena.

Chesapeake and Ohio Canal 1900-1928 © E.B. Thompson, Public domain

Diary entries from a soldier in Maine recount unearthly noises heard by the company's pickets only a year after the battle. Mules pulling the boats through this area also exhibited signs of unease, as if spooked by an unseen presence. There are also accounts of spectral figures, including a red-bearded man and an African American woman, vanishing upon closer inspection. Additionally, sightings of a ghostly dog wandering through the woods and hedges alongside the canal have perplexed those who search for it, as it mysteriously disappears upon approach. Curiously, balloons have been known to refuse ascent into the night sky, as if bound by an unseen force.

At the heart of the canal's mystique lies the infamous Paw Paw Tunnel, a structure shrouded in darkness and plagued by a tragic past. Construction of this tunnel began in 1836 and was initially expected to take two years to complete. However, due to various challenges, it took an astonishing 14 years to finish. The prolonged construction period led to mounting frustration among the workers, resulting in violent clashes between individuals of different ethnic backgrounds. Brawls, attacks, and even reported murders plagued the area, with local saloons and settlements falling victim to the chaos. The burning down of the lock house at lock 64, claiming the life of the lock keeper, stands as a haunting reminder of the tunnel's dark history.

Paw Paw Tunnel has become a focal point for paranormal enthusiasts, with persistent rumours of spectral activity within its depths. Legend has it that the tunnel is haunted by the tormented spirit of the ill-fated lock keeper. Visitors and investigators alike have reported witnessing unexplained shadows, hearing disembodied whispers, and experiencing unexplained phenomena.

Chesapeake and Ohio Canal National Historical Park © National Park Service Digital Image Archives, Public domain

In a captivating YouTube video by WooFDriver, an adventurous dog trainer, he and his group of explorers ventured into the Pawpaw Tunnel equipped with audio recording equipment. Among the recordings, a haunting whisper emerged repeatedly, mingling with the sounds of rushing water and eerie background music.

As one walks the towpath of the C&O Canal, encounters with the otherworldly are not uncommon. The darkened canal path sets the stage for an eerie walk, accompanied by mysterious sounds seemingly emanating from the unknown. Reports of apparitions, including an Indian chief and a spectral lady, add to the rich tapestry of spectral encounters that pervade the canal's haunted reputation.

Among the canal's folklore lies a tantalising rumour—a buried treasure concealed somewhere between Nolan's Ferry and the Monocacy River. Legends speak of a ghostly robber who materialises on moonless nights, crossing the Monocacy Aqueduct while carrying a lantern. Those who follow this ethereal guide are said to be led to the elusive riches, perpetuating the allure of hidden wealth along the C&O Canal.

The Chesapeake and Ohio Canal stands as a testament to the intertwining of history and the supernatural. With its rich heritage and haunting tales, this remarkable waterway continues to captivate the imaginations of those who seek a glimpse into its ghostly past. From the dark mysteries of Paw Paw Tunnel to spectral encounters along its towpath, the C&O Canal remains a compelling destination for those who dare to venture into its enigmatic depths.

Chapter 21

MASSACHUSETTS

Tragedy and hauntings aboard the USS Salem

The USS Salem, a Des Moines-class heavy cruiser, holds a captivating history that goes beyond its role as a vessel of war. Named after the town of Salem, this iconic ship was launched in 1947 and commissioned in 1949. It proudly served in the Atlantic and Mediterranean before being decommissioned in 1959. However, its story did not end there. Today, the USS Salem finds its resting place in Quincy, Massachusetts, near the very spot where it was built, serving as the United States Ship Building Museum.

During the Cold War, the USS Salem served as a symbol of peace, even though its guns never fired in combat. The mere presence of this mighty cruiser acted as a "stimulus for peace" in those tense times. However, beneath the surface, the ship holds tales of death, chaos, and tragedy that are nothing short of haunting.

One of the USS Salem's most significant deployments took place in 1953, when it was dispatched to the Greek Ionian islands to aid the victims of the Great Kefalonia Earthquake. This devastating earthquake ranks among the worst in Greek history, levelling numerous cities in Kefalonia and claiming the lives of over 500 people. The USS Salem transformed into a hospital and morgue, becoming a resting place for hundreds of earthquake victims. Many unfortunate souls never left the ship and are believed to wander its dimly lit hallways, searching for lost loved ones or their saviours. While large sections of the ship have been converted into museum displays, some rooms remain untouched.

USS Salem Museum © Sswonk, Public domain

One such room is the third wardroom, also known as the "mess hall," situated directly above the makeshift morgue, which essentially served as a large freezer. This particular area is rumoured to have the most paranormal activity. The USS Salem's connection to death is not limited to earthquake victims. During seismic events, gas lines can rupture and cause fires, leading to additional casualties. The presence of the ash scent reported by many visitors could be attributed to the number of fire-related deaths on the ship.

Among the spectres said to roam the USS Salem is The Burning Man, an apparition believed to have perished from severe burns suffered on the ship. Visitors and ghost tour guides often encounter this spirit in the room that once housed the ship's morgue. The same area is also said to be inhabited by a young Greek girl, a dark and taunting entity, and a menacing hellhound with a bone-chilling growl.

It is not only victims of tragedy who linger aboard the USS Salem. Several workers and sailors who served on the ship met their demise while fulfilling their duties. Some had been transferred to the Salem for medical care after being injured on other ships, only to pass away while on board. These spirits are also said to still wander the ship, forever connected to their final resting place.

USS Salem underway in the Mediterranean Sea on 16 June 1952 © Naval History & Heritage Command, Public domain

Among the many paranormal encounters aboard the USS Salem, one notable apparition is that of a man named John, who was a maintenance worker before his passing. John's ghost, the ship's first known tour guide, would appear to visitors in fully human form. His presence remained unknown until guests began praising the excellent, albeit nonexistent, guide.

Additionally, the ship's kitchen area is believed to be maintained and organised by the ghost of a former cook. On the other hand, the mess hall is plagued by the spirit of a man who disrupts the area by dragging and overturning chairs.

Peter Blumberg, a printer at the ship museum, experienced a chilling encounter while walking down a hallway near the ship's rear. A tall male figure materialised several feet in front of him, making eye contact before silently descending a staircase, seemingly uninterested in any human interaction. Similarly, other museum workers, including the ship's archivist, have reported hearing unexplained footsteps and voices calling out to them when no one else is present.

The paranormal activity aboard the USS Salem has attracted the attention of television shows dedicated to investigating the supernatural. Ghost Hunters, for example, captured EVP recordings of banging noises and what appeared to be a woman's voice. Unusually high electromagnetic field (EMF) readings have also been recorded, further adding to the ship's eerie reputation. The Travel Channel even recognized the USS Salem as one of the "most terrifying places" to visit.

For those daring enough, the USS Salem offers the opportunity to spend the night and embark on a personal paranormal investigation. This once-mighty warship now serves as a gateway to the mysteries of the afterlife, inviting visitors to explore its haunted corridors and uncover the truth behind the countless stories of lingering spirits.

Chapter 22

MICHIGAN

The Mysterious Paulding Light

The legend of the Paulding Light is an intriguing tale that hails from Paulding near the Michigan border with Wisconsin. It is believed to have originated in 1966 when witnesses first caught sight of an enigmatic light that appears in a valley outside of the small town. According to local lore, the light is said to emanate from a swaying lantern held by the ghost of a railway brakeman who tragically lost his life while attempting to halt an oncoming train. Since then, the legend has grown, captivating the imaginations of locals and visitors alike.

Numerous explanations have been proposed over the years in an attempt to demystify this phenomenon. Some suggest that the light stems from a nearby highway, originating from automobile headlights. Other theories propose that it could be attributed to swamp gas, extraterrestrial activity, or even the spirit of a grandparent searching for a lost grandchild. Seismologists say a few small earthquakes left some small cracks in the ground that let out radioactive gases, which could cause the light effect. Yet, despite these conjectures, the source of the Paulding Light remains elusive, teasing researchers and fueling speculation.

The allure of the Paulding Light has turned the town's abandoned gravel road into a popular tourist destination. Eager visitors flock to catch a glimpse of the infamous light, often referred to as the Pulled-In Light. Recognising the growing interest, the US Forest Service has erected a sign to discourage littering and guide enthusiastic sightseers to the best vantage points

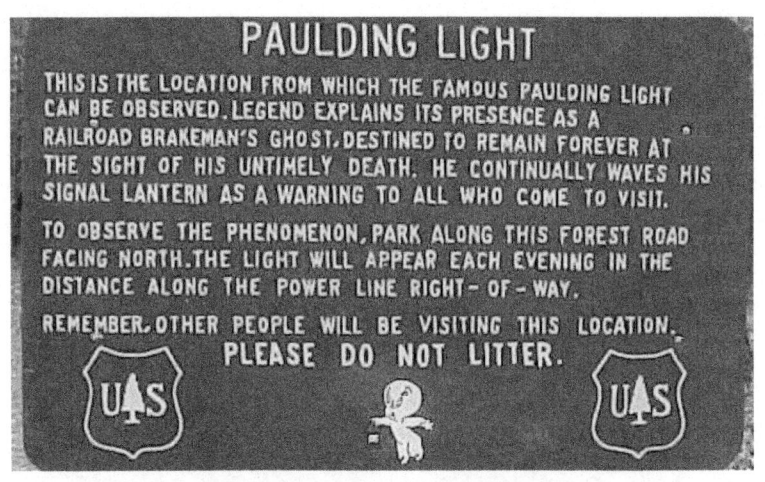

Paulding light sign © https://www.ontonagonmi.com

Over time, the legend of the Paulding Light has taken on a life of its own, magnified by accounts and anecdotes passed down through generations. However, it is important to approach these stories with a healthy dose of scepticism. Eyewitness testimony, though intriguing, can be influenced by mass hysteria and subjective experiences. In 2010, a group of determined students attempted to solve the enigma surrounding the light, driven by a desire to uncover the truth behind the legend.

Several experiments were conducted in an attempt to unravel the mystery of the Paulding Light and determine its origin. These investigations aimed to provide scientific explanations for the phenomenon but, thus far, have been unable to definitively solve the mystery.

One common experiment involves observing the Paulding Light using advanced equipment such as spectrographs and telescopes. Researchers have recorded the light's characteristics, such as its colour, intensity, and movement patterns. These observations aim to gather objective data that can be analysed and compared to known light sources or natural phenomena.

Another approach involves measuring the electromagnetic radiation emitted by the Paulding Light. By using specialised devices, scientists have attempted to detect any unusual electromagnetic activity in the vicinity of the phenomenon. This experiment seeks to determine if the light's source is related to any known electromagnetic sources or if it exhibits unique properties.

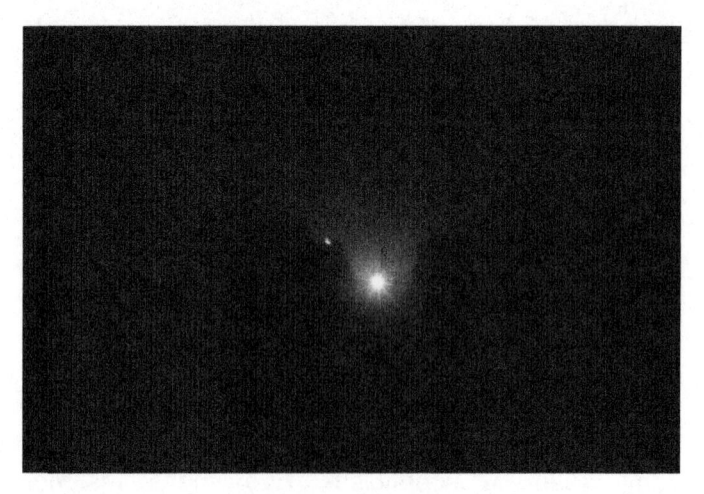

Paulding Light © Flivver 99 at English Wikipedia, CC BY 3.0

Furthermore, researchers have explored the possibility of atmospheric conditions or natural phenomena playing a role in the creation of the Paulding Light. For instance, some experiments have focused on studying the presence of swamp gas, which can sometimes produce luminous effects in certain conditions. By analysing the composition of the air and the specific conditions present during the sightings, scientists aim to identify any correlation between the light and natural atmospheric phenomena.

Additionally, efforts have been made to rule out artificial light sources as the cause of the Paulding Light. Researchers have conducted experiments to study the positioning and movements of cars or other artificial light sources in the vicinity of the observation area. These experiments help determine if the light can be attributed to headlights or other artificial sources that might be mistakenly perceived as supernatural.

The scepticism surrounding science and paranormal experiments is also worth noting. Many people feel that scientific explanations strip away the enchantment and mystique surrounding phenomena like the Paulding Light. This scepticism becomes evident when faced with self-funded experiments aimed at replicating paranormal activity.

All in all, the Paulding Light remains a perplexing local mystery in Michigan. Its unexplained nature and the stories shared by visitors at the nearby Running Bear Resort only add to its allure. The light's visibility from a distance of eight miles serves as a constant reminder that there are still enigmas in the world waiting to be unravelled, beckoning us to explore the realms beyond the known.

Chapter 23

MINNESOTA

Anoka, the Halloween Capital Hauntings

In the realm of eerie festivities, there exists a place shrouded in mystique and renowned as the Halloween capital of the world. Found in the heart of Minnesota, a state brimming with seasonal spirit, Anoka emerges as a beacon of Halloween revelry, captivating locals and visitors alike with its enchanting allure. But beyond the surface-level merriment lies a tapestry of chilling tales and haunted histories, one of which centres around the infamous Anoka State Hospital and its rumoured paranormal activities.

Minnesota's claim to Halloween fame can be traced back to its distinction as one of the first cities in the United States to initiate a grand-scale celebration of the spooky holiday. A tradition that began with a festive parade and gradually evolved into a city-wide extravaganza teeming with ghoulish delights for children. For the residents of Anoka, this annual spectacle serves as more than mere entertainment. It serves as a diversion, offering an outlet for their exuberant energies while diverting them from trouble and mischief.

It was during this time that the city's government and local businesses came together to initiate a grand Halloween celebration, complete with parades and festivities. This marked a significant shift, as the town decided to embrace the spirit of Halloween and create a citywide extravaganza. Thus, the seeds of Anoka's transformation into the Halloween Capital of the World were sown, forever altering the fabric of this extraordinary place.

While Halloween merriment became the town's trademark, Anoka also harbours a shadowy underbelly brimming with paranormal occurrences. One such location is the State Hospital, now known as the Anoka Mental Regional Treatment Center. It was a mental health facility notorious for its less-than-ideal conditions, leaving patients discontented with their stay. Former employees recount unnerving experiences within the hospital's labyrinthine network of tunnels. Voices echoing through the corridors seemed to shout, urging them to flee. These tunnels, originally intended for staff to navigate the premises efficiently, now carry whispers of the past, a haunting testament to the desperation of patients who sought escape from their confinement. The energy within the tunnels is palpable, evoking an unnerving sense of foreboding that keeps many staff members at bay.

Another haunting presence looms over the Anoka County Workhouse, claiming its rightful place among the top three most haunted workhouses in the United States. This accolade, although macabre, paints a vivid picture of the ominous atmosphere that pervades the building. Workhouses of the 18th and 19th centuries were known for their mistreatment of individuals, often resulting in tragic and untimely deaths. The Anoka County Workhouse stands as a sombre reminder of those troubled times, where suffering and neglect were distressingly common.

In the heart of Anoka, we find the Anoka Masonic Lodge, yet another site steeped in spectral tales. Shadows flit across the hallways, while whispers of ethereal voices penetrate the stillness. These stories reverberate throughout the lodge, igniting the imagination and curiosity of those who dare to tread within its walls. These spectral encounters contribute to the rich tapestry of paranormal phenomena that Anoka has become synonymous with.

Colonial Hall and Masonic Lodge No 30 © McGhiever, CC BY-SA 3.0

However, the focal point of our exploration lies within the walls of a building now known as Billy's Barn Grill. Despite its current incarnation as a lively bar and grill since 1987, this structure has served various purposes throughout its long history. From an elegant hotel to a French restaurant, an apartment complex to a gathering place for prohibition-era parties hosted by local banks, this building has witnessed the passage of time in its many guises.

During its time as the Jackson Hotel in the late 1800s and early 1900s, one particular room became the haunt of a spectral presence—an innocent little girl. Paranormal investigators ventured into the room, guided by a sense that a playful spirit lingered within. To their astonishment, during an EVP (Electronic Voice Phenomenon) session, they asked the young apparition if she wished to play. Clear as day, a disembodied voice responded, requesting them to sing the nursery rhyme "Ring Around the Rosie." The hair-raising moment unfolded before their eyes, leaving an indelible mark on their psyches.

Emanating from the building's kitchen, eerie occurrences further cement the ethereal reputation of Billy's Barn Grill. Tables have been rearranged, seemingly prodded by unseen forces, while the staff would return to find the place impeccably set despite having left it bare the night before. An unseen presence, potentially that of a former waitress, displays a phantom helping hand, dutifully preparing the dining area. The apparition of a woman in white has also materialised in the dining room, vanishing when one turns to gaze back at her seat. This inexplicable phenomenon has repeated itself, perplexing both staff and patrons alike.

Jackson Hotel © McGhiever, CC BY-SA 3.0

It is advised to never venture upstairs or descend into the basement alone, as strange occurrences often transpire in these isolated spaces. However, sometimes curiosity supersedes caution. One brave investigative team ignored these precautions and found

Pursuit of the Paranormal

themselves pursued by an unseen force while exploring the basement of Billy's Barn Grill. The sensation of being relentlessly chased compelled them to flee, their heartbeats pounding in their ears as they raced up the stairs, feeling an unseen presence nipping at their heels.

Such spine-chilling encounters have cemented Anoka's reputation as the Halloween Capital of the World. The haunted tales that have woven themselves into the town's identity beckon intrepid explorers, daring them to uncover the mysteries that lie hidden beneath the surface. So, if ever you find yourself in the vicinity of Anoka, prepare to immerse yourself in a realm where Halloween transcends mere costume and candy, and the paranormal lingers in the shadows, waiting to be discovered.

Chapter 24

MISSISSIPPI

The King's Tavern Hauntings

In the heart of Natchez, Mississippi, lies a relic of the past known as the King's Tavern Building. Standing proudly for 237 years, this historic structure, also referred to as the King's Tavern, holds within its walls a captivating history intertwined with tales of paranormal phenomena.

During the Spanish settlement in the 1700s, the King's Tavern Building had its humble beginnings as a block house for Fort Panu. Constructed in a time when the frontier town lacked a sawmill, the building's sturdy beams were salvaged from scrapped sailing ships in New Orleans and transported to Natchez by mule.

As the years unfolded, the King's Tavern became a hub for various characters of questionable repute. Mercenaries, drunkards, and outlaws, including the infamous Harp Brothers, frequented this establishment. Known for their sadistic acts of torture and murder, these outlaws would return to Natchez after their misdeeds, indulging in their ill-gotten gains while lodging at the King's Tavern.

King's Tavern © Ralph Clynne, Public domain

Throughout its long history, the King's Tavern changed hands multiple times, serving different purposes. It transitioned from a private dwelling to a bed and breakfast, a hotel, and a tavern. In 1973, the building was sold and restored as a tavern and restaurant, reclaiming its original name, the King's Tavern. Over the years, countless individuals, both residents and travellers, have crossed its threshold, adding their own stories to the tapestry of this extraordinary place.

Within the dark annals of the King's Tavern's history, certain gruesome events have left an indelible mark. One such incident involves Big Harp, one of the Harp Brothers, who, while staying at the tavern, brutally murdered a baby in the attic room then went back to the bar to order another drink.

Another tragedy unfolded in the life of Richard King, the owner of King's Tavern. Seduced by the allure of a young server named Madeline, Richard embarked on a passionate affair, forsaking his marital vows. The discovery of their illicit liaison by Richard's wife led to a chilling act of vengeance. Madeline's fate remains shrouded in mystery, as she was either killed by hired thugs or met her demise at the hands of Richard's wife herself. Her body, along with two others, was concealed within the chimney wall of the tavern's main room, a grim secret hidden from the world.

In the 1930s, when renovations were underway, the shocking revelation of mummified bodies occurred. Among them were the remains of Madeline and the two men, possibly victims of the same violent forces that silenced her. As the bodies were respectfully laid to rest, a potent energy was stirred within the building, awakening restless spirits and giving rise to a surge of paranormal activity.

Visitors and staff of the King's Tavern have encountered spectral phenomena that defy explanation. Shadowy apparitions glide through stairways, while the fireplace emanates heat as if kindled by unseen hands. Footprints appear on recently cleaned floors, shocking those who witness them materialise across wet surfaces. Most notably, witnesses including both guests and staff, have attested to the appearance of a young woman who bears a striking resemblance to the ill-fated Madeline. Madeline's presence at the King's Tavern has become one of the most compelling and frequently reported paranormal encounters within the establishment.

Described as beautiful and engaging, Madeline's apparition manifests in front of startled individuals, often leaving them in awe or unsettled by her otherworldly presence. She seems to linger within the tavern, perhaps unable to escape the tragedy that befell her all those years ago.

However, unlike vengeful spirits or malevolent entities, Madeline's nature appears to be mischievous rather than malicious. She engages in a series of playful pranks, as if seeking attention or interaction from the living. Jars and objects are mysteriously knocked off shelves, and water cascades from the ceiling onto the floor in a seemingly controlled manner. Chairs hanging on walls have been observed rocking with an inexplicable force.

The staff and visitors have also reported strange occurrences surrounding doors and lights. Doors that were closed and locked suddenly swing open, responding to Madeline's name when called, only to shut again as if under her command. Lights flicker and dim, their illumination manipulated by an unseen force, leaving witnesses astounded and awestruck.

Natchez MS 1850's © Henry Lewis, Public domain

Madeline's presence has transcended the visual realm and made its way into audio recordings as well. An electronic voice phenomena (EVP) captured by a paranormal investigation team within one of the empty bedrooms contains a faint yet distinct cry for help. While the exact circumstances surrounding this plea remain unknown, it adds another layer of intrigue to Madeline's enigmatic presence within the King's Tavern.

Her significance within the paranormal landscape of the tavern cannot be understated. As one of the victims whose tragic demise became entwined with the building's history, Madeline serves as a poignant reminder of the lingering impact of past events. Through her playful antics and occasional cries for help, she continues to make her presence known, ensuring that her story and the history of the King's Tavern remain forever intertwined.

Beyond Madeleine's mischievous nature lies a more sinister presence that permeates the depths of the King's Tavern. Reports from paranormal investigators describe a malevolent entity donning a top hat. Its origins remain shrouded in mystery, with speculation ranging from murder victims to the very outlaws who once frequented the tavern. Witnesses recount unsettling encounters with this malevolent force, experiencing an overwhelming sense of evil and enduring aggressive paranormal activities. Some claim to have glimpsed the face of a man peering through a mirror in one of the upstairs bedrooms, forever trapped in the spectral realm.

The King's Tavern's haunted reputation persists, as staff and guests continue to share spine-chilling encounters. Whispers of a baby's cry reverberate through the halls, even when no children are present. Hair-pulling, unexplained pushing, and mysterious bedroom lock-ins have left their mark on those who have dared to venture within. This hallowed structure, constructed from repurposed timber hailing from New Orleans' sailing ships, serves as a conduit for the tormented souls of the Harp brothers and other outlaws who once terrorised innocent victims.

As the oldest building in Natchez, the King's Tavern stands as a testament to the city's vibrant history. From its humble beginnings as a fortification to its current incarnation as a haunted tavern, this remarkable structure has woven together the tales of rogues, lost souls, and spectral apparitions. The echoes of the past continue to reverberate within its walls, drawing visitors to experience the intriguing blend of history, mystery, and the ethereal that can only be found within the hallowed halls of the King's Tavern.

Pursuit of the Paranormal

Chapter 25

MISSOURI

Shadow Folk of Avilla & the Haunted Death Tree

Avilla, a charming small town nestled in Jasper County, Missouri, boasts a population of merely 103 residents, as recorded during the 2020 census. Founded back in 1856, this idyllic town was once an integral part of the renowned Route 66, which played a pivotal role in boosting tourism in the region. Although Avilla is no longer connected to the iconic route, it still retains its status as one of the cherished "living ghost towns of Route 66." Presently, it stands as a serene farming village, adorned with county homes and picturesque farm houses scattered across its countryside.

Now, let's delve into why Avilla has earned the title of a "living ghost town," encompassing two intriguing aspects.

Firstly, Avilla truly embodies the essence of a ghost town, with its sparse population and numerous abandoned structures that stand as eerie reminders of the past. As you stroll through the town, you'll come across empty buildings, and if you look closely, you'll find a solitary shop, a bar and grill, and a post office comprising the essence of the town. Notably, not all the streets are even visible on online street view platforms, suggesting that some of the deserted lanes have been overlooked by digital mapping services.

AvillaMO © Traveler7 CC BY-SA 3.0

Secondly, Avilla carries tales of actual apparitions and supernatural encounters, adding to its reputation as a haunt for ghostly phenomena. Local inhabitants caution visitors to exercise caution when exploring the empty residences, as sightings of enigmatic "shadow folk" have been reported. These spectral figures resembling darkened silhouettes of people—shadows without the presence of actual individuals—have been observed wandering through abandoned hallways, glimpsed through windows, and even spotted walking along desolate roads after nightfall.

Despite their mysterious nature, the shadow folk are regarded as benign entities by the locals. They seem disinterested in the living, leaving one to speculate that they are merely imprints of bygone inhabitants, frozen in time and space.

Among the supernatural occurrences in Avilla, the bar and grill known as "Bernie's" holds its fair share of spooky tales. The establishment's owner, Rick Walker, recounts an incident where all

Pursuit of the Paranormal

the pool cues inexplicably fell off the wall, defying logical explanation. These cues were firmly secured, leading Walker to consider the possibility of an external force, yet no one was present to cause such a disturbance.

Orbs, mysterious spherical shapes often associated with paranormal phenomena, have also been witnessed within the premises of Bernie's. Walker, even when alone in the bar after closing, sometimes experiences an uncanny sensation of being watched, prompting the hairs on his neck to stand on end. Despite these eerie encounters, he has grown accustomed to such ethereal presences.

AvillaPostOffice © Eric Swanger, CC BY-SA 3.0

However, the most renowned apparition in Avilla stems from a legend rooted in the Civil War era. Like many towns across the United States, Avilla endured its own division during this tumultuous period, resulting in a significant exodus of its residents.

The legend revolves around a spectre haunting the town, famously known as the "Avilla Phantom Bushwhacker" or "Rotten Johnny Reb," who not only haunts the town itself but also the ominous

"Death Tree." During the war, a Union patrol from Fort Scott, en route to join the local militia in Avilla, stumbled upon the lifeless body of a Confederate Bushwhacker. Rather than providing a proper burial, the soldiers opted to hang the decapitated skull from a tree as a deterrent to other bushwhackers. The skull remained suspended for over a year, serving as a macabre warning.

As a result, the ghostly figure of "Rotten Johnny Reb" emerged, described as a headless apparition frequently donning a duster coat and sometimes clutching a rifle or lantern. The restless spirit tirelessly roams the town and surrounding woods, forever searching for his severed head and seeking vengeance against "Yankees" to avenge his demise. Over the years, numerous deaths were attributed to this infamous legend, causing many of the remaining townspeople to flee, their spirits dampened by the eerie spectre of "Rotten Johnny Reb."

Regrettably, the exact whereabouts of the Death Tree have become lost to the annals of time, as the countryside surrounding Avilla has undergone considerable transformations, with woodland and forests forming a perplexing labyrinth of changing landscapes.

Chapter 26

MONTANA

Bannack: A Forgotten Gold Rush Town

Bannack, Montana, a desolate ghost town with a chilling past, holds the remnants of a bygone era. Once the territorial capital of Montana, this abandoned settlement was a thriving gold mining town that attracted prospectors from all corners of the world. In this podcast episode, we delve into the fascinating story of Bannack, uncovering tales of corruption, gang-related murders, and paranormal encounters that continue to intrigue visitors to this day.

Established in 1862 and named after the local Bannack Indians, the town flourished upon the discovery of gold. At its peak, Bannack boasted a population of approximately 10,000 residents who were drawn to the area in search of fortune. However, beneath its glittering facade, the town harboured a dark underbelly.

Bannack's history is marred by tales of lawlessness and violence. Sheriff Henry Plummer *(Inset)*, entrusted with maintaining order, was accused of leading a notorious band of road agents responsible for over 100 murders. The allegations prompted swift action from the vigilance committee, resulting in Plummer's execution, along with that of two of his deputies. Subsequently, 22 individuals faced trial and met a similar fate at the hands of the vigilant citizens.

One of the most notorious landmarks in Bannack is the Hotel Mead, a place where history and paranormal activity intertwine. Echoes of the past reverberate through the walls of this historic building, with reports of eerie occurrences and unexplained phenomena. Visitors have recounted hearing the sounds of crying children, possibly remnants of the days when the hotel served as a hospital. However, the focal point of the hotel's haunting is the spirit of Dorothy Dunn, the daughter of a former manager, who met a tragic end by drowning. Witnesses claim to have spotted Dorothy in various parts of the hotel, including guest rooms and the balcony. She is often described as a spectral figure donning a blue dress, her presence leaving an indelible impression on those who encounter her. Moreover, cold spots and the presence of other entities suggest that Dorothy is not alone in haunting the Hotel Mead.

Indeed, the hotel is said to harbour multiple spirits, each with their own story to tell. Alongside Dorothy, an older woman and orbs have been sighted, leading to speculations about the hotel's haunted past. Countless guests have come and gone, some perhaps never truly leaving, as their spirits remain tied to this historical landmark.

Furthermore, other buildings in the vicinity, including a nearby museum, have also been reported to have paranormal activity.

Bannack's turbulent past extends beyond the realm of the supernatural. As a small town thriving during the gold rush, it became a magnet for wealth and corruption. Rumours of a million-dollar fortune in gold circulated, attracting gangs and corrupt officials who sought to exploit the riches. This influx of unsavoury characters left an indelible mark on the town's history, contributing to its eventual abandonment in the 1970s.
Inset: Hotel Meade in Bannack Montana © Woolsterp, CC BY-SA 4.0

During the era of the Wild West, Bannack, like many other gold towns, became a hub for poker and gambling. The allure of the gold rush brought together businessmen and newly wealthy individuals who sought to test their luck at the card tables. In fact, Bannack's connection to gambling was so significant that a popular television program, "My Terror Town," even explored a neighbouring ghost town called Gunslinger Gulch, known for its association with gold and gambling.

Bannack is just one of many ghost towns scattered across the Midwest and the middle part of the United States. These eerie remnants of the past stand as testament to the transitory nature of human settlement and the fleeting dreams that once thrived within their borders, leaving as quickly as they arrived.

Bannack © Mr Hicks46, CC BY-SA 2.0

In contrast to the United Kingdom, where land ownership is more centralised, ghost towns in the United States often fall under the jurisdiction of local councils. This difference in land governance contributes to the swift turnover of residents and the abandonment of these once-vibrant settlements.

As we explore the ghost town of Bannack, Montana, we are reminded of the ephemeral nature of human endeavours and the echoes of the past that continue to resonate. Bannack stands as a haunting reminder of a bygone era, a testament to the resilience of history and the enduring allure of the paranormal.

Chapter 27

NEBRASKA

Hauntings and the Devil at Hummel Park

Hummel Park, located in Omaha, Nebraska, is renowned as one of the state's most haunted destinations, captivating visitors with its scenic beauty spanning over 200 acres. Legends suggest that this picturesque park may have once served as an ancient Native American burial ground, adding an intriguing allure to its mystique.

The park's landscape features steep hills and meandering dirt paths, offering an adventurous experience for those who explore its terrain. Along the eastern edge, a notable area known as the "Devil's Slide" garners attention due to its history of unfortunate suicides. Erosion has shaped the landscape into steep cliffs and precipitous drop-offs, adding to the sombre ambiance.

Tragically, during the early 1900s, the park became associated with a darker chapter in its history when it was allegedly used for lynching. Disturbingly, the claims are that numerous black individuals were hanged from the trees that line the entrance road, casting an eerie shadow over the park. Witnesses have claimed to see the ghostly apparitions of these victims still hanging from the trees, their desperate cries echoing through the night. It is believed that the weight of their tormented souls and the haunting memories of their gruesome deaths cause the trees to bow even to this day.

Among the park's enigmatic phenomena is the legend of the "Morphing Stairs," a long stone staircase situated at the park's highest point. Mysterious in nature, these stairs appear to defy a definitive count, with individuals recounting different numbers when ascending and descending. According to one fable, if one were to successfully count the same number of steps in both directions, it is foretold that their demise is imminent. Alternatively, another legend suggests that the devil himself will manifest and offer a wish to anyone who accomplishes this feat, but at the cost of their soul.

MorphingStairs © Adam Fletcher Sasse, NorthOmahaHistory.com

The "Morphing Stairs" lead down a steep hill, revealing a valley that houses a deteriorating shelter known as "the Devil's Den." Sinister symbols such as inverted pentagrams and swastikas, along with the presence of deceased animal carcasses, hint at occult rituals and devil worship that may have occurred within Hummel Park's bounds. While the park's connection to a Native American burial ground and malevolent spirits remains unverified, the tangible evidence of satanic altars adorned with writings serves as a chilling testament to the park's eerie ambiance.

Tragically, Hummel Park has also witnessed numerous instances of violence, including notorious murders. One such case involved Laura LaPointe, an Omaha prostitute who, in 1983, fell victim to sexual assault and robbery at the hands of four fellow prostitutes. She met a grisly fate, beaten to death with a six-foot tree limb and a softball bat, her lifeless body eventually discovered in a roadside ditch concealed within the park's densely wooded area.

HummelPark © Dj Romm13, CC BY-SA 4.0

In another harrowing incident, the remains of 12-year-old Amber Harris, missing since the previous winter, were uncovered in a shallow grave in Hummel Park in 2006. Additionally, the park became the site of a fatal car accident in 2008, claiming the life of a young man named David Murillo.

Hummel Park's legends continue to thrive, with tales of an albino colony deep within the woods persisting since the 1950s. Although no official records or photographic evidence substantiate these claims, eyewitnesses swear by the existence of a secretive group of albinos who have made the park their home.

Lastly, nestled within the park, a small lodge serves as a gathering space for families but has suffered from vandalism and damage over time. Curiously, those who have ventured into the lodge have reported an uncanny presence accompanying them, while photographs have captured unexplained orbs, further heightening the eerie atmosphere.

Visitors to Hummel Park frequently encounter disembodied screams and cries, lending credence to the park's reputation as a paranormal hotspot. Local ghost hunters have reported anomalous electromagnetic readings and witnessed various ghostly apparitions, indicating a significant level of otherworldly activity permeating Hummel Park's grounds.

Chapter 28

NEVADA

Secrets of the Luxor Hotel in Las Vegas

The Luxor Hotel in Las Vegas stands as an iconic pyramid-shaped resort, captivating visitors with its Egyptian-themed allure. From its massive structure to the powerful beam of light illuminating the night sky, the Luxor has become a prominent landmark on the famous Las Vegas Strip. However, behind its grand facade lie stories of construction errors, fatal incidents, and an eerie aura that has sparked rumours of paranormal activity and curses. In this article, we delve into the enigmatic history of the Luxor Hotel and explore the intriguing events that have shrouded it in mystery.

When Circus Circus Enterprises conceived the Luxor Hotel, they sought to create a resort that would captivate both children and adults. Inspired by ancient Egypt, the hotel aimed to transport guests into a world of pharaohs and pyramids. Standing at three-quarters the size of the Great Pyramid of Giza, the Luxor became the third-largest pyramid in the world. Its unique design and mesmerising beam of light became immediate attractions, drawing visitors from far and wide.

Luxor Hotel © Iconoteca dell'Accademia di architettura CC BY-SA 4.0

Despite its remarkable appearance, the Luxor Hotel's construction was not without its troubles. Cost-cutting measures played a significant role in the hotel's development, leading to fatal construction errors. Built at half the cost of neighbouring establishments like the Mirage, the Luxor's construction process was rushed and incomplete. Tragically, this resulted in accidents and deaths that forever stained the hotel's history.

The rush to complete the Luxor Hotel had dire consequences. Workers fell victim to fatal accidents, with some losing their lives during the construction process. These untimely deaths seemed to have left an otherworldly imprint on the hotel. Many reports and eyewitness accounts speak of paranormal activity within the Luxor's walls. Ghostly apparitions of construction workers and a prevailing sense of bad luck have become part of the hotel's enigmatic reputation.

Beyond the realm of the supernatural, the Luxor Hotel has witnessed a series of unfortunate incidents that have left a lasting impact. From fatal jumps to deadly altercations, these incidents have added to the hotel's mystique. A woman tragically lost her life after jumping from the 26th floor, her identity unknown. Other incidents include a man falling from the 10th floor and an employee who was killed by a homemade explosive device concealed in a coffee cup. Furthermore, a fatal fight erupted between a former football player and a mixed martial artist during a party held in a Luxor suite. The consequences were devastating, leading to a tragic loss of life.

Luxor Hotel Lobby & Rooms © Rob Young CC BY 2.0

The Luxor's history is intertwined with tales of curses and ill fortune. Some attribute this dark cloud to the hotel's location on a former mobster burial ground. Belief in the mystical properties of the pyramid shape and its ability to attract negative energy adds to the sense of foreboding. Moreover, Luxor's design, reminiscent of a tomb, has been associated with bad luck according to certain cultural beliefs. These factors have contributed to the pervasive notion that the Luxor Hotel is cursed.

Multiple rooms have become home to a recurring presence: a mysterious blonde woman whose intentions remain unknown, whether for business or pleasure. One unmistakable pattern emerges, however—the Luxor Blonde exhibits a peculiar affinity for strangulation, not upon herself, but rather toward unsuspecting guests occupying her bed.

Numerous visitors have reported awakening to a terrifying sensation of hands tightly gripping their necks, gasping for breath and overwhelmed with fear. Yet, upon inspecting their surroundings, they find no trace of an intruder.

Interestingly, many of these affected guests have mentioned being in the midst of a dream before their unsettling encounter, with the central figure consistently being the enigmatic blonde woman.

Curiously, the paranormal phenomena appear to be more prevalent in the pyramid section of the Luxor, compared to the tower-filled areas, as witnessed by vacationers who have experienced these eerie events.

Not all hotel guests catch a glimpse of the Luxor Blonde, but they often wake up grappling with breathlessness, racing hearts, and with sweat on their pillows and sheets. Even those without any previous heart issues have suffered severe chest pain while staying here.

The Luxor Hotel in Las Vegas remains an enigmatic testament to both grandeur and mystery. Its pyramid structure, powerful beam of light, and Egyptian theme continue to captivate visitors. However, behind the facade lies a troubled history filled with fatal construction errors, tragic incidents, and reports of paranormal activity. The Luxor's allure is undeniable, drawing people in with its mystical charm. Yet, it stands as a reminder that even the most mesmerising destinations can carry an air of intrigue and darkness. The Luxor Hotel will forever be etched into the annals of Las Vegas history, a testament to the mysteries that lie beneath its surface.

Chapter 29

NEW HAMPSHIRE

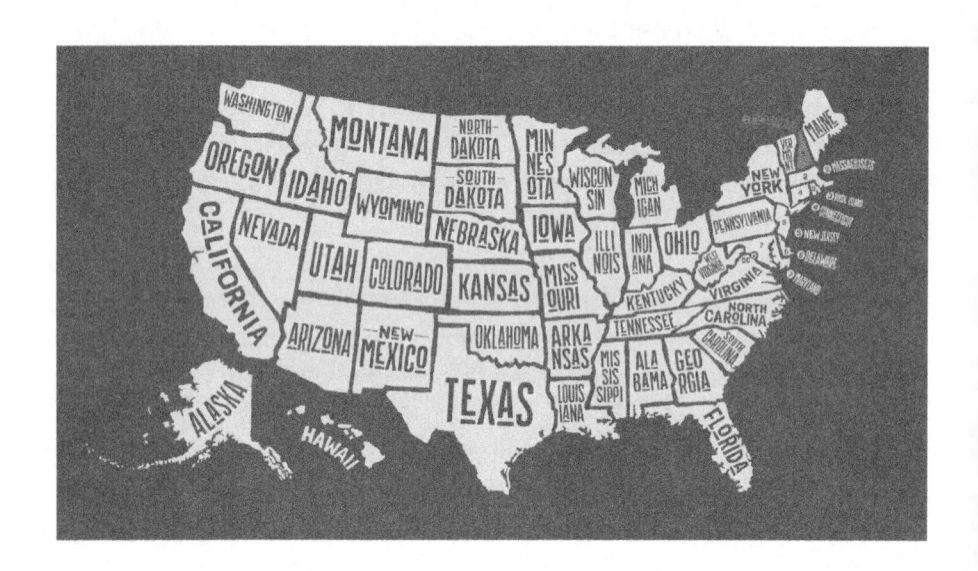

The Haunted James House of Hampton

Located in Hampton, near Portsmouth, New Hampshire, stands the James House, a remarkable testament to American history. Constructed in the year 1723, this colonial building holds a sense of age that is truly unparalleled. As a genuine "first period" colonial structure, it proudly retains its original framework, a rare feat indeed.

Benjamin James, a prosperous farmer, became the proud owner of this land in 1705. Remarkably, the James family maintained ownership of the property for an astonishing 226 years. However, in 1931, the Campbell family acquired the house after the passing of the last James family member. Due to the Campbell family's ill-health and their son's unfortunate demise, they were unable to continue operating the farm. Sadly, with no remaining heirs to inherit the estate, it was deemed necessary to part ways with the property.

Since its vacancy in 1972, the James House has experienced a new lease on life. In 1994, the James House Association was established by concerned neighbours who wished to prevent the historic dwelling from falling into disrepair. Today, the house serves as a museum and offers educational tours, providing insights into its rich history and the lives of its former residents.

Given the extensive history of this ancient structure, it comes as no surprise that numerous ghost stories have circulated throughout the years. Skip Webb, the president of the James House Association, has personally encountered the presence of a ghost on three separate occasions. One particularly chilling incident involved a guest fleeing the house during a tour, terrified after claiming to have witnessed a ghost. In 2001, a hymnal, typically found in churches and containing hymns, inexplicably fell from the ceiling. Such occurrences have solidified the house's reputation as a paranormal hotspot. Additionally, neighbours have reported glimpses of ethereal figures within the windows.

BenjaminJamesHouse © Magicpiano, CC BY-SA 4.0

Local paranormal investigators known as Spirit Chasers Paranormal have dedicated several years to studying the James House. They assert that they have obtained compelling evidence of otherworldly happenings while staying at the property. During their initial visit, they managed to capture numerous photographs featuring orbs, which they believe to be signs of spirits attempting to materialise visibly. They have also heard peculiar noises, such as a ball seemingly bouncing down the stairs to the ground floor, despite no physical object being discovered. Furthermore, there have been instances of loud bangs against the exterior walls, only for no source of the noise to be found. One particular night, they heard a loud bang on a different wall, accompanied by what appeared to be the sound of someone sawing inside the house, despite no one being present. Their most chilling encounter occurred on Halloween night when they captured an Electronic Voice Phenomenon (EVP) of a woman laughing. This laughter did not belong to any member of their small team. In their report, they documented additional phenomena, including a forceful door slam, taps on the walls, and other unexplained sounds.

For those intrigued by the enigmatic occurrences at the James House, the James House Association offers regular investigations that visitors can participate in. Moreover, during Halloween, a special event is held, featuring seances and an outdoor ghost hunt, providing an exhilarating experience for enthusiasts and thrill-seekers alike.

I would like to conclude by briefly mentioning another intriguing haunted house located in Hampton. This particular dwelling is known as the Marston House and is rumoured to be haunted by the ghost of Valentine Marston, an 11-year-old boy who tragically accidentally shot himself with his father's gun in 1890, resulting in lead poisoning which caused his untimely death.

During the 1950s and 1960s, numerous sightings of a young boy were reported, particularly in houses owned or previously owned by extended members of the Marston family. Interestingly, Valentine is described as a "white ghost," and those who have encountered him claim to experience positive occurrences in their lives.

One remarkable account involves a family residing in a former Marston house on Tide Mill Road. They had been struggling to sell the property when a peculiar incident took place. As the lady of the house was hanging her laundry outside, she suddenly felt a hand gripping hers. To her astonishment, she looked down to find a young boy dressed in a sailor suit and hat, smiling at her. In an instant, the boy vanished into thin air. Later, when shown a photograph of Valentine by a local teacher and historian, she positively identified him as the boy she had seen. Astonishingly, within less than 48 hours of this encounter, the house was successfully sold.

Chapter 30

NEW JERSEY

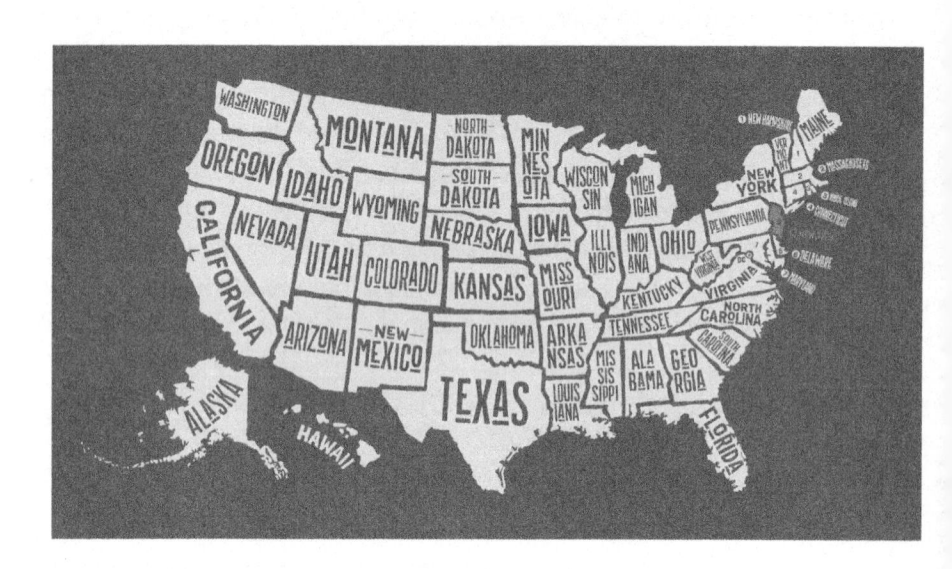

Cryptids, Ghosts, and the Jersey Devil

Deep within the heart of New Jersey lies the enigmatic Pine Barrens, a vast forest that has gained a reputation as one of the most haunted locations in North America. Spanning an impressive 1.1 million acres, this mysterious woodland is not only home to a multitude of ghostly apparitions but also harbours a rich history dating back to 1200 AD and boasts an array of ghost towns, more than any other state, and supernatural creatures.

Designated as a national reserve in 1978, the Pine Barrens serves as a protected haven for its unique ecological system. However, it is the paranormal phenomena that have captured the fascination of many who dare to explore its depths. Tales of ghosts and spectres abound in this sprawling forest, contributing to its eerie allure.

One of the most infamous legends associated with the Pine Barrens is that of the Jersey Devil, a cryptid creature that has fascinated locals and intrigued paranormal enthusiasts for centuries. According to the lore, the Jersey Devil was born in 1735 as the thirteenth child of Deborah Leeds of the Leeds family, who were early settlers in the region. It is often described as a flying creature with hooves and a goat-like head, possessing large bat-like wings, a horse-like body, a long, forked tail and a spine-chilling scream, the creature instils fear in the hearts of those who dare to speak its name. The creature is also known by other names such as the Leeds Devil.

Reports of sightings of the Jersey Devil date back to 1820, but it was the events of 1909 that sparked widespread panic and hysteria. In response to the numerous claims of encounters with the creature, a ten-thousand-dollar bounty was offered for its capture. While no firm evidence of the Jersey Devil's existence has been found, its terrifying depiction in sketches and descriptions has cemented its status as a legendary entity. Some describe the Jersey Devil as a harbinger of disaster, while others claim it preys on livestock and pets. The creature is often associated with strange sounds, footprints, and eerie occurrences in the Pine Barrens.

Jersey-Devil © Various/several, Public domain

Pursuit of the Paranormal

The legend of the Jersey Devil has become deeply ingrained in New Jersey folklore and popular culture. It has inspired various books, movies, and even a professional hockey team, the New Jersey Devils.

The Pine Barrens is not limited to the Jersey Devil, however, as it is teeming with various other legends and apparitions. Stories of wandering spirits and supernatural occurrences have become intertwined with the forest's fabric. It is said that the ghost of a young boy haunts Burnt Mill Road, forever seeking justice for his untimely demise after being killed in a hit-and-run. If you drive down the road at night, you may just see a boy running for his ball..

Another spirit said to roam the area is the ghost of James still, an African American Doctor during the time of slavery, lynched when locals found out that he was practicing medicine. He is said to be a friendly ghost, assisting those lost or needing help in the area, carrying on his medical duties

In addition to its spectral inhabitants, the Pine Barrens also bears witness to historical tragedies. One such memorial within the forest pays tribute to Emilio Carranza, a Mexican aviator who tragically crashed during a storm. Carranza, on a mission for peace, met his untimely end in the Pine Barrens. The Carolina Memorial stands as a solemn reminder of his ill-fated flight.

Beyond the depths of the Pine Barrens, New Jersey itself harbours a plethora of urban legends. Locals recount tales of encounters with the Jersey Devil at Lucille's Country Cooking diner, while the Cedar Bridge Tavern is said to be haunted by the spirit of John Wildemoth, a former owner who delights in mysteriously opening and closing doors.

Interestingly, even buildings that have fallen into disrepair have their own stories to tell. One such structure, abandoned and left to decay, was eventually restored to its former glory. However, the restoration process was not without its peculiar occurrences. Footsteps echoing through empty hallways and the laughter of children, despite the absence of any visible presence, have left many pondering the lingering spirits that may still reside within.

The Pine Barrens of New Jersey, with its ghost towns, supernatural creatures, and haunted history, continues to captivate the imagination of those who dare to delve into its depths. Whether a sceptic or a believer, the allure of the unknown beckons curious souls to explore the mysteries concealed within this bewitching forest.

NJDevil © Philadelphia Evening Bulletin, January 1909, Public Domain

Chapter 31

NEW MEXICO

Hauntings of Fort Stanton

Fort Stanton, situated just outside the town of Lincoln, NM, has a rich and diverse history. Constructed in 1855, its primary purpose was to safeguard the hispano and white settlements along the Rio Bonito during the Apache wars. Throughout the years, the fort has served multiple roles, including functioning as an army post, a tuberculosis sanatorium, an internment camp, and even a correctional facility.

In 2008, an exciting announcement was made regarding the future of Fort Stanton. Plans were unveiled to transform it into a living history venue, leading to a series of improvements and renovations over the following decade. Dedicated volunteers played a crucial role in constructing living quarters and exhibits, giving the fort a renewed sense of purpose.

However, like many buildings with such extensive history, Fort Stanton carries a darker side. Numerous accounts of deaths, murders, and suicides have taken place within its walls, leaving an eerie imprint on the premises. Visitors and workers alike have reported spine-chilling encounters, further adding to the fort's mystique.

Fort Stanton - Unknown author, Public domain

The Lincoln County Paranormal and Historical Society has conducted thorough investigations and interviews with individuals connected to the fort and its surrounding area. These findings have been meticulously documented on their website, shedding light on the paranormal experiences recounted by numerous witnesses. Here are a few notable encounters:

1920s - Reports emerged of shadowy figures and inexplicable crying within the administration building. One anonymous individual shared, "Indian drums and flute music is what I heard and no one could have been there because it was a guaranteed clean up."

In the 1930s, a janitor named Emanuel Beltron, who had previously dismissed the existence of ghosts or paranormal phenomena, experienced something profoundly unsettling on his very first night working at Fort Stanton. In his own words, he claimed to have seen "El Diablo sus solo" – the devil himself. Fearing for his life, Beltron resigned from his job the following morning. Astonishingly, this wasn't the only report of encountering the devil. In the 1970s, during the fort's time as a women's prison, an inmate described seeing a figure so sinister that she believed it to be the embodiment of the devil.

During the 1940s, when the fort held 80 Japanese prisoners of war, disturbing reports surfaced of maltreatment and abuse by the guards. Records indicate 24 suspicious deaths and 37 documented suicides. In 1948, a woman named Connie Montes, who worked in the administration building, had a chilling experience. While she assumed a passing shadow was a mere mouse, she was startled when something grabbed her hair and forcefully pulled her back into her chair. She screamed, but the entity persisted until she began praying. Despite her fright, Connie decided to continue working at the fort, always wearing a protective rosary, and never encountered a similar occurrence again.

Maria Montoya, a worker during the 1950s, along with other employees, frequently witnessed shadows, heard voices, and experienced other inexplicable phenomena. These eerie encounters occurred throughout the day, mainly within the gymnasium, administrative buildings, and occasionally in the cafeteria. Another office worker, Heidi Greer, shared that they consistently discovered open drawers and cabinets in their office, even though everything had been left neat and organised the night before. However, the most unnerving aspect for Heidi was the repeated instances of hearing her name being called in a deep, raspy voice.

One area that attracts considerable interest is the morgue, as expected. Tomas Frujillo, another employee, found himself in the morgue when he heard a ghostly whisper in his ear saying, "Tomas, you're coming with us." He suddenly felt an intense heat on his leg, described as so hot that it felt cold. To his astonishment, upon inspecting his leg, he discovered three distinct claw-like marks, each approximately eight inches in length. Terrified, Tomas rushed upstairs, where he inexplicably felt as if he tripped over an unseen obstacle.

Officers Quarters Fort Stanton © AllenS, Public domain

Lily Hardy, who worked at Fort Stanton during its tenure as a mental facility in the 1980s and 1990s, often heard peculiar noises emanating from the morgue. These sounds resembled banging on the ceiling and screams, although they didn't resemble ordinary human screams. Instead, they possessed a lower pitch, adding to the unnerving atmosphere.

The accounts of paranormal encounters at Fort Stanton are undeniably fascinating, particularly the striking similarities observed across decades. From appearances of the devil to unidentified voices calling out workers' names, the fort's history is steeped in mysterious and haunting occurrences.

Chapter 32

NEW YORK

The House of Death

The House of Death, located in Greenwich Village, is a seemingly ordinary townhouse with an extraordinary reputation. This unassuming residence is said to be inhabited by not just one or two, but a staggering 22 spirits.

Built in 1856, this historic townhouse has a dark and mysterious past. Originally owned by James Boorman Johnston, the founder of the Metropolitan Underground Railway, the house took on the moniker of the House of Death due to a series of unfortunate events that unfolded within its walls. After Johnston's passing, his widow and children moved into the house, unaware of the dark fate that awaited them.

One famous occupant of the House of Death was none other than the renowned writer Mark Twain. Struggling with financial difficulties and battling depression, Twain found himself seeking solace within the private confines of a house on West 10th Street. It was during his stay here that he encountered a potentially supernatural occurrence involving a piece of firewood mysteriously moving on its own. He pulled out his gun and shot it, assuming that the wood was being moved by a rat. The shot produced drops of blood, which he assumed was rat blood, but no other evidence of a rat, or rats in the building, was found. Twain moved out about 12 months later with the house becoming occupied on and off over the coming years and in 1937 the building was converted from a house into a number of apartments.

Mark Twain © A.F. Bradley, Public domain

Jan Bryant Bartell, an actress and writer, claimed to have had numerous spiritual encounters while residing in this home and went on to write a book detailing her 12 years of experiences entitled 'Spindrift: Spray From a Psychic Sea'.

Some of these encounters included feeling as if eyes were looking at her when she was alone, something brushing against her neck but there would be nothing there, and a rotting stench intermittently, appearing and disappearing unnaturally quick. The family dog would act aggressively towards a particular chair in the room, leading them to believe that a spirit favoured the chair to sit in. Jan even claimed to have seen a full bodied apparition which she touched and explained the sensation as being damp or cold and like moving through a fog or a cloud.

Eventually she was disturbed enough to seek the assistance of a spirit medium and a paranormal investigator. The medium claimed to have felt a presence beneath the floorboards, and during one encounter, she allegedly became possessed by the spirit of a young woman. Whilst in the trance, the spirit told them she was born in 1848 and that her husband died in the civil war.

One of the most reported phenomena in the House of Death is that of the woman in white, a young woman wearing a nightgown or dress and is said to wander through the halls of the House of Death, walking through walls and doors, leaving an eerie and unsettled atmosphere in her wake. These disturbances have even spread to neighbouring houses, further amplifying the reputation of the haunted residence.

Joel Steinberg, a New York criminal defence attorney and resident of the building in the 1980s, became infamous for his involvement in child abuse and ultimately the death of a child, perhaps the most horrifying incident associated with the House of Death. On November 1st, 1987 his daughter, 6 year old Lisa, was tragically found lifeless and unclothed on the kitchen floor, while the son endured a distressing existence, restrained in his playpen in a soiled diaper. There were also a lot of drugs found close by, including marijuana ,cocaine and crack pipes.

Lisa was taken to hospital but never regained consciousness and died three days later with her cause of death judged to have been the result of blunt force trauma to the head. The subsequent investigation revealed a disturbing pattern of abuse inflicted by Joel upon his wife, daughter, and son Mitchell, along with the illegal adoption of the two children.

As the stories and legends surrounding the House of Death grew, reports of ghostly apparitions and unexplained phenomena multiplied. Mark Twain's ghost is said to have made an appearance in the Greenwich Village home, despite having not lived at the property for that long. His spirit has been witnessed by multiple residents walking up and down the stairs and in the 1930's a woman and her daughter who lived there claimed that a spirit introduced himself by the name of Clemens, Mark Twain's real surname.

Mark Twain House © Ajay Suresh CC BY 2.0

The House of Death stands as a testament to the enduring fascination humans have with the supernatural. It serves as a reminder that even within the most ordinary facades, there can lie a world of secrets, spirits, and unexplained phenomena. As long as the tales of the House of Death continue to be shared, the spirits that reside within its walls will never be forgotten, forever imprinted in the paranormal history of New York City.

Chapter 33

NORTH CAROLINA

The Haunted Tar River

The Tar River, a meandering waterway that spans across northeastern North Carolina, gracefully flows into the Pamlico Sound lagoon on the eastern coast of the United States. Renowned as a historical route for Tar-carrying barges, the river winds its way through numerous quaint towns in the region. Interestingly, the name of the river originates from its significance in the transportation of Tar.

According to a tale documented by random-times.com, an English immigrant named Dave Warner arrived in the area during the Revolutionary War era and established a mill on the Tar River. Dave, who empathised with the cause of the newly emerging nation, utilised his grain supplies to aid the young army. With his imposing stature, characterised by jet-black hair and a long beard, he possessed robust arms and legs, honed by the arduous task of lifting massive bags of flour.

In August of 1781, a resident of the town rode to the mill with an urgent warning for Dave: the British troops were in close proximity and had learned of his affiliation with the rebels. Advised to shut down the mill and hide, Dave Warner laughed off the suggestion, expressing his determination to stay and confront the British intruders, perhaps even exacting his revenge upon them. Regrettably, when the British soldiers arrived and forcibly entered the mill, they discovered both the miller and the messenger desperately trying to salvage every ounce of grain they could. Overwhelmed by the red-coated troops, Dave, despite his formidable strength, succumbed to their superior numbers.

Tar River © U.S. Department of Agriculture, Public domain

Legend has it that the soldiers executed Dave on the banks of the Tar River, subsequently casting his lifeless body into the water near the long-vanished port village of Old Sparta. As his blood infused the river, turning it crimson, Dave vowed to the soldiers that he would seek vengeance upon them, declaring that each of them would be visited by a Banshee, a harbinger of their impending demise. Convinced by his chilling words, the soldiers agreed to kill the miller, chaining him to heavy stones before immersing him in the depths of the Tar River.

Now, what exactly is a Banshee? Derived from Irish folklore, the term "Banshee" translates to "fairy woman" in Old Irish. A Banshee is a female spirit known to foretell the death of a family member through mournful wailing, shrieking, or keening. When the Banshee's haunting cry resonates, it signifies that a family member has recently passed away or is on the verge of doing so, even if they are located far away. The Banshee's wail serves as an ominous warning to the household. Additionally, the Banshee is considered a harbinger of death, and her piercing screams serve as an alert that an individual is about to enter a situation where survival is unlikely.

Banshee © W.H. Brooke, Public domain

Shortly after the patriot's warning, all three of the British soldiers found themselves abruptly awakened by the sorrowful wails of a female apparition, the Banshee herself. She forewarned them of their imminent demise in battle. As fate would have it, all three soldiers met their tragic end, shot and killed during a skirmish near the town of New Bern shortly thereafter.

Legend has it that the Banshee never departed from the Tar River following these events. It is believed that she now haunts an area near the city of Tarboro. According to the tales, anyone who ventures into the waters where the patriot, Dave Warner, met his untimely end over two centuries ago, particularly during the month of August, risks encountering the Banshee. She will wail into the night, prophesying their forthcoming death.

Therefore, if you happen to find yourself near the Tar River in Tarboro, North Carolina, on a moonless night when the river resembles inky blackness and a thick mist hangs in the air, it is advised to steer clear. The Banshee herself may manifest, her chilling cries echoing through the night, serving as a haunting reminder of the legend that continues to capture the imagination of locals and visitors alike.

Moving on to another sinister story from Tarboro... the gruesome history of the Mayo house. According to local lore, Mr. Mayo, a former resident of the house, succumbed to a fit of rage, committing a horrifying act that would forever leave an imprint on the property's history. In an unspeakable act, he murdered his entire family, including their beloved pet dog.

After coming to his senses, and seeing the bloodbath around him, Mr Mayo, not believing what he had just done, was so shocked and distraught that he then took his own life by hanging himself in the house.

Legend has it that when you enter the garden of the property, the ghost of the dog will meet you and point you towards the front door where the family are waiting for you, but as soon as you enter the house, the door will slam suddenly behind you and the family have disappeared, leaving only the noose with which Mr Mayo used to hang himself.

As visitors explore Tarboro's historical landmarks, they are reminded that the past holds more secrets than meets the eye. Whether one is drawn to the town's historical significance, the majestic Tar River, or enticed by the spine-tingling allure of Mayo House, Tarboro offers a unique and hauntingly memorable experience for all who venture within its boundaries.

Chapter 34

NORTH DAKOTA

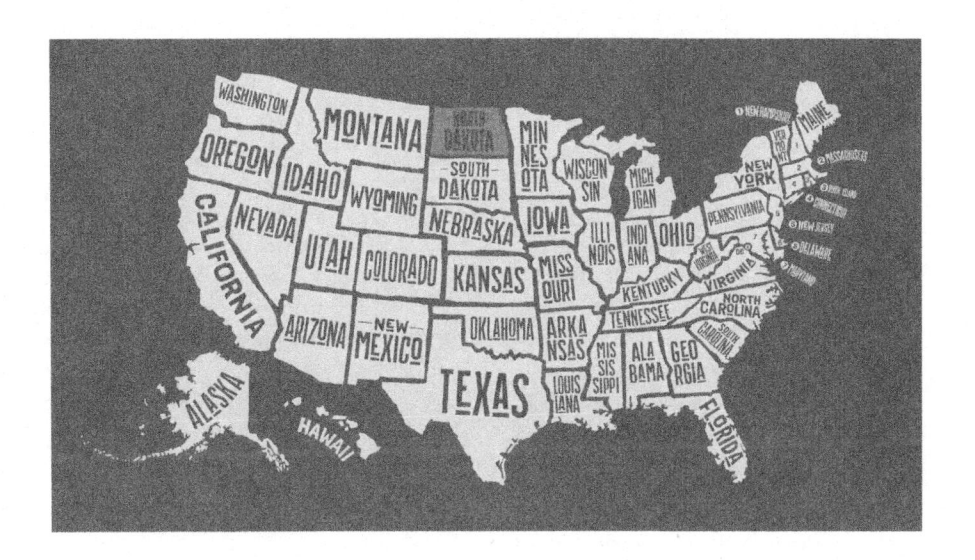

Beyond The San Haven State Hospital

North Dakota, known for its tranquil landscapes and unassuming charm, harbours a secret realm that few dare to speak of - a world where the paranormal intertwines with reality. In this captivating journey into the supernatural, we delve into the chilling hauntings that infest the nooks and crannies of this unsuspecting state, shedding light on some of the most notorious locations where the veil between the living and the dead grows thin.

Located in Bismarck, the state library building holds not only a wealth of historical knowledge but also a host of paranormal occurrences. One notable incident involved James Sperry, the former superintendent of the historical society, and his loyal canine companion, Shadow. Late one evening, as James was working in his second-floor office with Shadow by his side, the atmosphere took a sinister turn. Suddenly, Shadow started growling and bolted down the hall, heading straight for the basement. A few moments later, a terrified Shadow returned, tail between his legs, leaving James puzzled as to what had frightened his faithful companion.

Public library, Bismarck, N. Dak ©Tichnor Bros.Inc, Public domain

Another spine-tingling encounter occurred when James took an elevator to the basement. To his surprise, he saw a man in a white shirt enter a storage area with only one entrance. Curiosity got the better of him, and James followed the man into the room, only to find it empty when he turned on the lights. The mysterious figure had vanished, leaving James perplexed and unsettled.

In a separate incident, a former archivist named Lis Vaneen was working overtime with a colleague named Craig Gannon. As they toiled away in the sub basement, Lis distinctly heard a voice call his name: "Come here, Lis." Assuming it was Craig, he followed the voice through the stacks, only to discover Craig two floors above, completely unaware of the eerie call that had summoned him.

The former governor's mansion, situated in an undisclosed location in North Dakota, is known for its spectral manifestations. One of the most active areas for paranormal activity is the old master bedroom, where a former governor named Briggs met his demise. Visitors and staff have reported witnessing doors opening and closing on their own within the master bedroom and curtains have been seen swaying mysteriously, even when there is no breeze present. Closet doors, known for their large and heavy build, have also been observed opening and closing without any human intervention.

Another common occurrence in the mansion is the sound of footsteps on the staircases. Both staff and visitors have reported hearing phantom footsteps over the years, particularly on the staircase leading to the basement and the one ascending to the second floor and attic.

It is worth noting that the former Governor's Mansion is a place of historical significance, reflecting North Dakota's rich political heritage. Whether you believe in ghosts or not, the stories and encounters associated with this haunted location contribute to its cultural and historical significance, adding an air of mystery and intrigue to its already notable past.

San Haven Sanatorium, now known as the San Haven State Hospital, near Dun, was initially established in 1909 as a treatment facility for tuberculosis patients. Over time, it transformed into a residence for individuals from the former North Dakota Institute for the Feeble-Minded. The dilapidated building, which has fallen into disrepair, carries a haunted reputation. Urban legends and tales surround San Haven Sanatorium, with reports of unusual occurrences attributed to the spirits of those who suffered from tuberculosis or mental illnesses during the institution's operational years

Apparitions are frequently sighted, with witnesses claiming to have seen ghostly figures wandering the halls and rooms of the sanatorium. Strange noises, including disembodied cries of babies, have been heard echoing throughout the abandoned corridors, defying rational explanation. Visitors also describe an overpowering feeling of being watched or accompanied by unseen entities. This sensation, coupled with the building's deteriorating condition, intensifies the sense of dread and apprehension among those who dare to step foot inside.

San Haven, North Dakota licensed under CC BY-SA 2.0

The fifth floor of the sanatorium, in particular, has gained a reputation for being exceptionally eerie. It is said to exude an almost palpable energy that sends shivers down the spines of even the most intrepid individuals. Legends and myths circulate about the fifth floor, including a tragic tale of a trespasser falling down an elevator shaft and meeting an untimely demise.

North Dakota, a state often praised for its unspoiled beauty, conceals a haunting secret beneath its serene facade. These tales of paranormal encounters serve as a chilling reminder that sometimes, the line between the living and the dead blurs, leaving us with a sense of both trepidation and fascination for the unknown.

Chapter 35

OHIO

The Haunted Moonville Tunnel

Nestled in the scenic Brown Township of southeastern Ohio, the once-thriving mining town of Moonville sprang to life as the Marietta and Cincinnati railroad expanded its reach. What makes this town truly fascinating is its exclusive connection to the outside world—the Moonville Tunnel. Carved through one of the towering hills, this 50-yard brick tunnel, along with two trestles spanning the winding Raccoon Creek (the longest creek in the world), served as the sole access point to and from the town.

Intended primarily for train passage, the tunnel's construction harboured a fatal flaw—it was too narrow for pedestrians to navigate safely when trains rumbled through. As a result, the area became treacherous for those unfortunate enough to find themselves on the tracks as a train approached. Tragically, over 21 recorded deaths occurred on or near these tracks, with the most recent incident taking place in 1986, when a young girl met her untimely fate under the wheels of a passing train on the trestle.

Railroad workers dubbed this railway line the "most lonesome and desolate" due to its isolated nature and the unexpected arrival of trains. Today, Moonville exists only as a ghost town, its remnants reduced to the tunnel itself, a few bridge foundations, a cemetery, and the lingering spirits.

Moonville Tunnel © ChristopherM, CC BY-SA 3.0

Visitors and tourists exploring the area have shared chilling encounters with the apparitions of former railroad workers who met their demise in tragic accidents. Witnesses describe seeing these spectral figures waving their lanterns, forever bound to the tracks and the tunnel. Among them, two distinct ghosts make regular appearances, leaving an indelible mark on Moonville's haunted history.

One ghostly presence is attributed to Theodore Lawhead, an engineer for the Marietta and Cincinnati railroad company. Lawhead's spirit began haunting the tracks after a catastrophic head-on collision with another train in the 1880s. Visitors have reported sightings of a luminous figure, clutching a lantern, strolling alongside the tracks and through the eerie confines of the tunnel. An unnerving incident involving a group of rowdy youths in 1979 serves as a testament to the Engineer's ethereal existence. As they walked back from the local pub, the group spotted a flickering light trailing behind them. Assuming it was the sheriff on their tail due to their noise, two members of the group approached the light, only to realise it was an old-fashioned lantern, emitting an otherworldly glow. To their astonishment, no one was holding the lantern, which inexplicably swung back and forth.

Another ghostly resident, known as the Lavender Lady, has been encountered by numerous visitors near the Moonville Tunnel. Witnesses describe a frail, elderly woman walking alongside the trail, only to witness her sudden vanishing act, accompanied by a delightful waft of lavender scent filling the air. Local lore identifies this phantom as Mary Shea, an elderly community member who met her tragic end on the tracks near the far end of the tunnel. It is said that when her spirit returns, the unmistakable fragrance of lavender permeates the tunnel and its surroundings, a poignant reminder of her presence.

Madison County Bridge © Historic American Buildings Survey (HABS), Public domain

Among the apparitions haunting Moonville, the legend of the Bully casts its shadow over the town. Believed to be the ghost of Baldie Keeton, a Moonville resident with a reputation for belligerence when intoxicated, this spectre embodies the town's violent past. Legend has it that Baldie's favourite tactic was a crushing bear hug, often targeting individuals smaller and weaker than himself. One fateful night, after being ejected from a saloon following a fight, Baldie was discovered dead on the tracks near the Moonville Tunnel. While many suspect foul play, the circumstances surrounding his demise remain shrouded in mystery. The ghost of the Bully now gazes down upon unsuspecting visitors from above the tunnel, his menacing stare and occasional pebble throws perpetuating the legend. Terrified mothers once used tales of the Bully to caution their children against venturing out at night, lest they too fall victim to his spectral wrath.

Today, Moonville stands as an abandoned relic of the past, its tunnel and railroads transformed into a popular tourist attraction featuring hiking and biking routes. Since the final train passed through in 1988, visitors can now embark on a chilling journey through history, immersing themselves in the haunting ambiance of Midnight at Moonville, a Halloween and ghost-themed festival held on the old railroad bed and within the ethereal confines of the tunnel. As the moon casts its eerie glow on the forgotten town, the spirits of Moonville continue to weave their enigmatic tales, forever intertwined with the ghosts of the past.

Chapter 36

OKLAHOMA

The Satanic Purple Church

Deep within the outskirts of Oklahoma City lies the chilling tale of The Purple Church, a notorious addition to the state's collection of bone-chilling urban legends. Renowned as one of the most haunted places in the region, this foreboding site is believed to serve as a portal to the netherworld. Even the most intrepid seekers of the paranormal hesitate at the mere thought of venturing into this haunted abode. Prepare yourself for a glimpse into this eerie location, one that will undoubtedly make you think twice about approaching its ominous grounds.

Once the dwelling of a church, The Purple Church now stands as a relic of its former self, reduced to a concrete slab and a cryptic basement. Its name derives from the sinister purple pentagrams and spray-painted symbols that once adorned its walls, serving as macabre reminders of its eerie past. In an act of collective defiance, the local townsfolk eventually discovered the malevolent congregation that had taken up residence within its walls and swiftly razed the structure to the ground. While the remnants of the foundation and basement persist, something far more insidious has managed to elude destruction, defying the destructive forces of fire and all other attempts to eradicate it.

SatanicPurplechurch © Pull Over Adventures/Youtube

Another variation of the Purple Church legend veers away from its religious origins, suggesting that it was, in fact, an ordinary house rather than a place of worship, let alone a satanic one. As the story goes, the residence was once inhabited by a family that, over time, either succumbed to a tragic demise or simply vanished, leaving their dwelling abandoned. Whispers circulate about the family's lingering spirits, haunting the area and deterring any who dare trespass upon their ethereal domain.

Beyond its paranormal activity, The Purple Church harbours an unsettling reputation within the realm of the supernatural. It is rumoured to serve as a gateway to hell, a sinister abode that has drawn demons and malevolent spirits summoned by practitioners of Satanism and witchcraft throughout the ages.

Nestled inconspicuously within the desolation of a rural landscape, the basement of The Purple Church conceals a disconcerting aura, seemingly more than just an ordinary underground space. Accounts from witnesses recount numerous Satanic rituals taking place within the church's confines. Visitors report unsettling encounters, such as being touched or scratched by unseen forces, while eerie sounds echo through the halls. The annals of paranormal events associated with this site continue to grow, each more perplexing than the last.

According to local lore, during the nights of a full moon, satanic worshippers allegedly carry out sacrificial rites involving virgin or newborn victims within the vicinity of The Purple Church. Though unverified, the discovery of mutilated animals and scattered bones strewn across trees and makeshift altars along the path leading to the church adds a disturbing element to the tales.

Sean Sellers, a 16-year-old who infamously murdered his family in 1986, has been associated with The Purple Church's transformation into a site of Satanic worship, although these claims are speculative..

SatanicPurplechurch © Pull Over Adventures/Youtube

Numerous photographs have captured the presence of lifeless animal carcasses, lending credence to the claims of frequent animal sacrifices conducted at The Purple Church. Visitors often describe an overwhelming sense of foreboding, compelling them to flee the premises without hesitation. Compounding the eerie atmosphere, confrontations with disgruntled locals have become commonplace. Exhausted by the constant influx of thrill-seekers causing disturbances, these neighbours are known to take action, pursuing those who venture toward The Purple Church. Many have recounted being pursued by a black pickup truck devoid of headlights, leaving them to question whether the driver embodies a satanic entity or simply an exasperated resident.

Paranormal investigators, mediums, psychics, and ghost hunters who have braved the journey to explore The Purple Church recount tales of an overwhelming darkness that pervades the surroundings, its presence palpable and even audible. Rather than mere apparitions, these brave souls often attribute the sensations they experience to the presence of an otherworldly demon. Some investigators have stumbled upon live rituals in progress while exploring the site, bearing witness to shrouded figures, flickering torches, and the haunting echoes of chanting emanating from within the enigmatic confines of The Purple Church. In some instances, these unsuspecting individuals have even found themselves pursued by unknown forces, prompting hasty retreats from the foreboding grounds.

The legends surrounding The Purple Church, with its tumultuous past and enigmatic present, cast an indelible shadow over the small town of Spencer. Whether it is a testament to the enduring power of urban legends or a tangible link to the supernatural realm, this haunting location remains a testament to the enduring fascination with the macabre and the unknown.

Chapter 37

OREGON

The Haunted Oregon Trail

The Oregon Trail was a historic route used by pioneers and settlers in the 19th century to travel from the Missouri River to the fertile valleys of Oregon. It spanned around 2,000 miles through states such as Missouri, Kansas, Nebraska, Wyoming, Idaho, and Oregon.

The trail emerged as part of the westward expansion of the United States, as people sought new opportunities in the Oregon Country. It was primarily used from the 1840s to the 1860s, with the peak period occurring during the California gold rush in the 1850s.

Covered wagons, known as Conestoga wagons or prairie schooners, were used to transport belongings and supplies. Pioneers needed to stock up on provisions like food, water, tools, spare parts, and ammunition. Hunting, fishing, and trading with Native American tribes supplemented their resources..

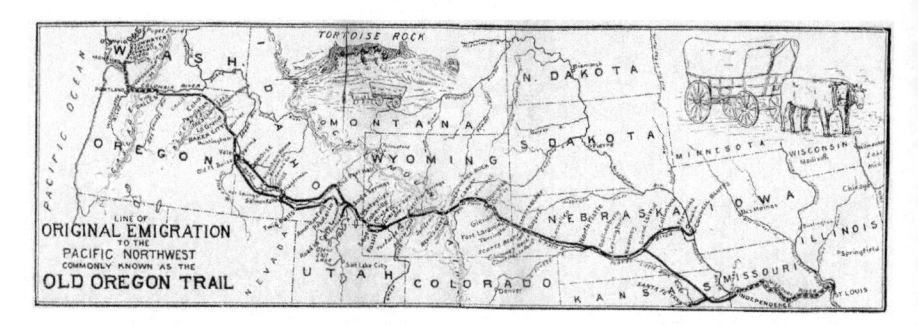

Old Oregon Trail 1852-1906 © Ezra Meeker. Fourth Edition 1907 Public Domain

Upon reaching Oregon, pioneers settled in different parts of the state, establishing farms, towns, and communities. The trail played a significant role in the westward expansion of the United States and the development of the American West.

Tragedies were a sombre reality along the trail. Disease outbreaks, particularly cholera, claimed many lives. Accidents, such as wagon overturns and river crossings, led to injuries and fatalities. Starvation and malnutrition were common due to limited food supplies, while exposure to harsh weather conditions caused illness and hypothermia. Native American conflicts, dehydration, and the physical toll of the journey further added to the hardships faced by pioneers.

It's estimated over 20,000 died at the roadside, buried in unmarked graves as the dead were quickly buried and the wagons moved on.

As a result, the Oregon Trail is dotted with gravesites and burial grounds, often marking the resting places of pioneers who perished during the journey. There have been reports of eerie occurrences and ghostly apparitions near these gravesites. Some witnesses claim to have heard whispers or cries, while others have reported seeing shadowy figures or experiencing feelings of unease and sadness in these locations.

Not far from Portland, Laurel Hill once posed significant dangers for travellers and the treacherous terrain often led to accidents, with wagons losing control and shattering into pieces at the bottom of the hill. Consequently, this infamous spot became a permanent resting place for weary emigrants to recuperate, tend to their injuries, and lay their departed loved ones to rest.

Among the tales spun by those who have visited the area are ghost stories that send shivers down the spine. One eerie account involves an old mess hall, where a door mysteriously swings open every morning around 4 a.m. It is believed that a spirit haunts the premises, starting its day by preparing breakfast.

In 2001, a group of volunteers made a remarkable discovery while excavating the grounds: a pair of graves concealed beneath a covering of rocks. Subsequent photographs revealed the presence of ethereal orbs hovering around the gravesite. Other inexplicable phenomena have been captured on film within the vicinity of the old bunkhouses, wherein peculiar glowing orbs manifest themselves.

The buildings themselves have been known to vibrate, as if a phantom presence were strolling by, even when no one else is present. A spine-chilling photograph portrays a woman's face eerily reflected in the mirror of an old piano, as if silently playing a spectral melody.

One particular cabin holds the spectral apparition of a woman in her late 20s or early 30s. This ghostly figure appears exclusively during rainy nights, gazing out of an upstairs window. If you happen to meet her gaze, she will offer a smile but remains silent, withholding any words.

Oregon City, the final destination for countless pioneers, holds a significant place in history. The spirits of the founding members still linger in some of the original and historic locations, adding to the city's rich past.

One such location is the Ermatinger house, a museum and one of Oregon's oldest buildings. A steamboat captain, a frequent guest, appears to have made the house his eternal abode. He continues to favour his preferred seat at the head of the dining room table, often pulling the chair out from under the table up to 20 times a day. This repetitive act annoys the current keepers, who are constantly pushing the chair back into place. Visitors have reported being touched by unseen entities, witnessing shadow figures wandering from room to room, and experiencing an unsettling feeling of being watched by an unknown presence.

Ermatinger House - Oregon City © Ian Poellet, CC BY-SA 3.0

Similarly, the McLoughlan house in Oregon City shares similar legends. John McLoughlan, the original owner, seems to still inhabit his former residence. Many guests and staff members have witnessed his presence, hearing his movements as he navigates the rooms, even ducking to pass through narrow spaces. His rocking chair regularly sways as if someone is sitting in it. In a rather eerie occurrence, every year on the morning of September 3rd, the face of John in a gold-framed oil painting hanging on the wall emits an eerie glow when the sunlight hits the frame.

Other encounters include a man feeling as if someone were choking him and attempting to push him towards the bannister of the stairs. Witnesses have observed a lady apparition dressed in a beautiful period gown ascending the steps. Additionally, displays that are beyond the reach of guests have been rearranged, and on one occasion, a cleaner vacuuming one of the bedrooms felt three taps on her shoulder. When she turned around to see who was there, no one could be found.

Chapter 38

PENNSYLVANIA

The Eastern State Penitentiary

The Eastern State Penitentiary is a historic former prison located in Philadelphia and was one of the first penitentiaries in the United States operating from 1829 to 1971. The prison's design and philosophy had a significant influence on the development of modern prison systems worldwide.

The prison was designed by John Haviland and is known for its distinctive radial floor plan. The layout consisted of a central hub from which seven cellblocks extended, resembling the spokes of a wheel. A design which allowed for better surveillance of the inmates. Once considered a groundbreaking institution, Eastern State Penitentiary served as a model for over 300 prisons worldwide, boasting an exorbitant construction cost of $800,000 during its inception, making it the largest and most expensive public structure ever erected in the United States at the time.

It was designed with the principle of separate confinement, emphasising the reform of prisoners through reflection and penitence. Inmates were held in single cells with high ceilings, providing them with their own exercise yard, private toilet, and a small skylight for natural light. The aim was to encourage inmates to reflect on their crimes and repent.

Eastern State Penitentiary © Carol M. Highsmith, Public domain

Various forms of restraints and devices were used to control inmates such as straitjackets, metal cuffs, and body belts. These devices restricted movement and were used to subdue unruly prisoners or those deemed a threat.

Other methods of punishment used at the prison making it a torturous hell included The "Mad Chair" or "Iron Gag" whereby prisoners were immobilised in a chair with tight restraints, placed in a way that forced the prisoner to maintain an uncomfortable and rigid posture for long periods. This punishment was used as a means of inflicting physical discomfort and humiliation.

Another disciplinary method involved submerging prisoners in a water bath known as the "Water Cure." The inmate would be strapped to a board and repeatedly dunked into icy water.

Over the years, Eastern State Penitentiary housed many infamous criminals, including Al Capone, the notorious gangster, who was incarcerated there in 1929-1930, on a concealed weapons charge. Other well-known inmates included bank robber Willie Sutton and Pep "The Cat-Murdering Dog" (a vicious hound sentenced to life for killing the governor's wife's cat), as well as James 'Big Joe' Bruno and several male relatives who were incarcerated there between 1936 and 1948 for the alleged murders in the Kelayres massacre of 1934

Rumours persist that Eastern State Penitentiary is haunted, with reports of ghostly encounters and inexplicable phenomena. However, it is worth noting that Ben Brookman, a tour guide at the prison, emphasises that the institution does not exploit its darker image, and the staff does not openly claim that it is haunted.

However, visitors and staff have reported seeing shadowy figures moving along the cell blocks and in the corridors of the penitentiary. These apparitions are often described as dark, indistinct shapes or silhouettes.

Many visitors claim to have heard unexplained whispers and voices echoing through the empty cell blocks. Some have even reported hearing their own names being called when no one else is around.

Cell block 12 is notorious for paranormal activity with visitors and staff having reported hearing disembodied laughter, weeping, and moaning coming from this area. Some have also experienced feelings of being watched or touched when entering the cell block.

Al Capone's cell, Cell 8, is a popular spot for paranormal enthusiasts. People have reported feeling a strange presence, cold spots, and even seeing Capone's ghostly figure sitting on the cot.

One of the most legendary tales comes from Gary Johnson, a locksmith who helped maintain the former prison. In the 1990s, Johnson worked to remove an old lock in Cell block 4, when he says "a force gripped him so tightly that he was unable to move. [It was] a negative, horrible energy that exploded out of the cell" in a blast of cold air. **(Inset:** *Cellblock 4 © Adam Jones, Ph.D., CC BY-SA 3.0)*

Within the confines of Eastern State Penitentiary, a chilling death ledger exists, bearing witness to the lives lost within its walls. Over a thousand entries chronicle the deaths of inmates, many of whom succumbed to suicide or illnesses such as tuberculosis. Interestingly, some archaic records even list "masturbation" as a cause of death for inmates in the 18th and 19th centuries, providing a glimpse into the strict moral codes that prevailed at the time.

While the Penitentiary harboured death row inmates within its notorious cell block 15, it never witnessed an execution. Instead, all inmates sentenced to death were transferred to the Pennsylvania State Correctional Institution for their final moments.

The harsh conditions and disciplinary methods used here in the past are now seen as part of the prison's historical legacy and a reminder of the evolving understanding of human rights and treatment of prisoners. Is it due to this history that causes the spirits to linger, forever trapped in the hell that was the Eastern State Penitentiary?

Whatever the reason, it becomes apparent that this foreboding structure holds within its walls a chilling past that continues to captivate the imagination, whether you believe in the paranormal or not.

Chapter 39

RHODE ISLAND

Ghosts & Haunted Pubs of Newport

Welcome to Newport, one of the oldest cities in the United States, founded back in 1639. We are about to embark on an exciting pub crawl through this historic town located in Rhode Island.

Our first stop is the renowned White Horse Tavern, believed to be the oldest tavern building in the country and the tenth oldest in the world. Constructed by English immigrant Francis Brinley in 1652, this tavern played a significant role during the British occupation of Newport in the American Revolution when it served as quarters for Tories and British troops.

After years of neglect as a boarding house, the White Horse Tavern was sold in 1952 and meticulously restored as a private tavern and restaurant. Today, it remains a popular destination for dining and enjoying drinks. However, this historic establishment is not without its ghostly tales. Legend has it that in the 1720s, a guest passed away in his sleep, causing great concern among the innkeepers who feared the spread of smallpox. Ironically, the innkeeper's sister, who was sent to the quarantine island of Coasters Harbour, contracted the disease herself but survived. The spirit of the elderly man, dressed in shabby colonial attire, is said to haunt the main dining room and occasionally bother female diners. Staff and guests have also reported encountering this apparition in the upstairs men's bathroom.

White Horse Tavern RI © Swampyank at English Wikipedia., CC BY-SA 3.0

Another spirit known to make its presence felt is believed to be a former staff member. This vigilant spirit watches over the staff, offering guidance and even reminding them to lock up, sometimes even earlier than usual. It patrols the building while the staff closes up for the night. Some speculate that this helpful spirit could be the same woman who is seen wandering around the tavern before vanishing near the fireplace.

Lastly, visitors have often heard the sound of a young girl crying, even though there are no children present. This mysterious sobbing, especially near the restrooms, remains unexplained, leaving guests intrigued by the supernatural occurrences at the White Horse Tavern.

Just across the street from the White Horse Tavern stands the Jailhouse Inn, which also has its fair share of eerie stories. Built in 1772, the building originally served as a jail and police station. However, in 2005, it underwent renovations and was transformed into an inn. Many original features, such as the old police check-in window and sliding iron bars in the dining area, were preserved to remind guests of the building's past.

On the third floor of the Jailhouse Inn, a strong presence is often felt, believed to be the spirit of a former jailer-in-charge who continues to oversee the premises and its occupants. Over the years, whispers from disembodied voices have been reported by both staff and guests, leading some to believe they are the conversations of former prisoners. Additionally, cold breezes are felt, even when doors and windows are closed and the weather is warm, adding to the mysterious atmosphere of the inn.

Ri-newport-jail-house © http://hauntedhouses.com

Leaving the Jailhouse Inn behind, our next stop is the Pilgrim House Inn, just a few streets away. Dating back to 1775, this bed and breakfast has been operating as an inn since the early 1800s. Among its spectral residents is the mischievous spirit of a young girl named Jessica. She is often seen gazing down from the windows onto the street and has been known to appear to guests in Room #8 and Room #11 on the third floor.

Legend has it that Jessica was the daughter of an Irish family who resided in the inn during the 1800s. She seems to take pleasure in playing pranks, such as buzzing intercoms in empty rooms, activating a music box in the dead of night, or even slamming the dryer door when the owner was loading laundry. During a Ghost Walk tour, a group reported sighting a little girl in an old-fashioned dress at the foot of the inn's stairs, despite no children being registered as guests that evening. Some speculate that Jessica's spirit lingers due to a tragic accident involving her falling down those very stairs.

Interestingly, the Pilgrim House Inn is known for its peculiar collection of stuffed rabbits. The innkeeper, Debbie Fonseca, began collecting toy rabbits, which eventually multiplied to occupy nearly every corner of the establishment. Could Jessica's mischievous spirit be drawn to these furry companions?

With each haunted tale, our pub crawl through Newport becomes an unforgettable experience, intertwining history, the paranormal, and the vibrant atmosphere of this charming city.

Chapter 40

SOUTH CAROLINA

The Old Charleston Jail

Charleston, South Carolina is a city known for its rich history and Southern charm. Among its many attractions, the Charleston Jail stands out as a haunting reminder of the city's dark past. From notorious criminals to ghostly apparitions, this jail has witnessed it all. Let's embark on a tour of this infamous institution and delve into the spine-chilling stories that surround it.

Constructed in 1802, the Charleston Jail served as a place of confinement for over a century, until its closure in 1939. Situated on land specifically designated for public concern, the jail played a central role in the city's law enforcement.

The Charleston Jail was not merely a prison; it also served other public functions. Within its confines, one could find a poor house, a hospital, and even a workhouse for slaves. Over the years, the jail underwent several renovations and expansions, with prominent architects such as Louis Bardot and John Sale leaving their mark on the building's design.

The Jail was also notorious for being the site of pirate executions and maintained a formal pirate court to prosecute and punish the pirates who had committed crimes on the high seas. Pirates actively plied their trade along the east coast of the US in the 18th and early 19th centuries and were prevalent in the Charleston area. To control piracy, the authorities held trials in the Charleston Jail and pirates were subsequently executed by hanging or other forms of summary punishment. There is a plaque in the gardens which states that thirty pirates were hung there in the gardens of the jail, and their bodies buried on the spot, a reminder of the city's struggle against seafaring criminals.

Old Charleston Jail © Warren LeMay from Covington, KY CC0

One of the most notable inmates in Charleston Jail was Lavinia Fisher, the first female serial killer in the United States. Imprisoned within the walls of Charleston Jail, she shared her captivity with a host of other nefarious individuals.

Lavinia and her husband, John Fisher, were infamous for the murders committed at their inn, known as the Charleston Inn Six Mile Wayfarer house. Guests who stayed at their establishment mysteriously disappeared, prompting complaints to the local sheriff. However, it took some time for action to be taken against the Fishers.

The couple's modus operandi was chillingly calculated. Lavinia would serve unsuspecting travellers tea laced with poison, weakening them. In their vulnerable state, John would strike, stabbing the victims to ensure their demise. Their belongings would be stolen, and the bodies were callously disposed of. The Six Mile Wayfarer house harboured an even more sinister secret — the bed in Lavinia's quarters was rigged to collapse, plunging unsuspecting travellers into a pit filled with deadly spikes.

As part of a criminal gang, they were both convicted of highway robbery and after an appeal were sentenced to death. According to legend, Lavinia used her last breath to scream, "If any of you have a message for the devil, tell me now, for I shall be seeing him shortly." Then jumped off the stand and killed herself. Her ghost is believed by some to haunt the Old Charleston Jail House, and tourists still claim sightings of her ghostly apparition

Rumours of Lavinia's diabolical activities at the Six Mile Wayfarer house have swirled throughout the years, making it challenging to discern fact from fiction. Nevertheless, the tales surrounding this chilling establishment serve as a testament to the horrors that transpired within its walls.

As well as sightings of pirates and Lavinia Fisher, there have been multiple reports of other spooky phenomena occurring. Including:

Witnesses have reported seeing objects move or disappear on their own throughout the jail. Chairs and other furniture have been reported moving in closed rooms, and even keys have been said to move on their own. It is also common for people to hear the doors to the cells and cells' heavy iron gates slam shut on their own;

Disembodied voices speaking to visitors, despite being alone. Some even claim to have heard screaming or the sounds of prisoners moaning in agony. Interestingly, many workers on several occasions have found human footprints in the dust of the jail cells, as if someone was walking around;

The ghost of a former prison guard has been seen patrolling the third floor in a spectral form. Some describe seeing his ghostly apparition with a lantern in hand, checking to make sure that everything is in order.

No matter the veracity of these famous stories… Whether they are reminders of the jail's dark past or the lost souls still lurking in the jail, there's no denying that the Charleston Jail holds a certain frightful appeal offering a chilling glimpse into a haunting chapter of South Carolina's past.

Chapter 41

SOUTH DAKOTA

Deadwood

Deadwood is a historic town located in the Black Hills of South Dakota. It was founded in 1876 during the Black Hills Gold Rush quickly became a thriving centre for gold mining, gambling, and general debauchery.

Deadwood's most famous resident was probably Wild Bill Hickok, a famous gambler and gunslinger who was killed in the town in 1876 by Jack McCall who shot him whilst playing poker at Saloon #10, giving rise to the famous term "Dead Man's Hand" of Aces and Eights which Wild Bill was holding when he was killed. Today, visitors to Deadwood can see a recreation of the saloon where he was shot, as well as a statue of Hickok himself on the town's main street.

In addition to its Wild West history, Deadwood is known for its legalised gambling, which was reintroduced in 1989 in an effort to revitalise the town's struggling economy. Visitors can enjoy slot machines, blackjack, poker, and other games at several casinos in town.

Main street deadwood © Richie Diesterheft from Chicago, IL, CC BY 2.0

Deadwood is also located near several popular tourist attractions, including Mount Rushmore, the Crazy Horse Memorial, and the Badlands National Park. The town itself has a number of historic buildings, shops, and restaurants that cater to visitors who come to experience its unique history and culture.

The Bullock Hotel located on Main St, Deadwood is a historic property that was built in 1895 by Seth Bullock, a famous sheriff and entrepreneur in the town. The hotel's architecture is distinct for its Italianate style and ornate detail.

Over the years, the property has been used for a variety of functions, including a hotel, a boarding house, even a brothel. The building fell into disrepair in the mid-20th century but was purchased by new owners in the 1980s and underwent extensive renovations to restore its historic charm.

One of the most well-known ghosts of the Bullock Hotel is the spirit of Seth Bullock himself. After dying of cancer in 1919, he is said to have never left and his tall, ghostly figure has been seen in various areas of the hotel, including the basement, and the restaurant where plates have been known to shake and fly off the tables. Lights and appliances turn on and off by themselves, unseen hands move items as well as water fixtures turning on on their own. One story tells of parents that couldn't find their young son and, after frantically searching the hotel, they returned to their room to find the boy happy and healthy. He told them he'd left to get a soda and got lost, but a nice man helped him find his room. When the family went to check out the next morning, the boy identified the helpful man — by pointing at a portrait of Bullock.

Many guests have reported hearing their name called out by a male voice when no one is present or tapped on the shoulder by unseen hands. Others have heard whistling, and many report the sounds of footsteps in the hallways when no one is there.

In both the second and third floor rooms, guests have reported several strange occurrences, including photographs that produce strange anomalies, alarm clocks that go off, even when they are unplugged, televisions that seemingly operate on their own, shadowy figures seen in rooms and hallways, and even an antique clock, that hasn't functioned in years, that chimes of its own accord.

The nearby Fairmont Hotel also has its own creepy history. Previously a brothel and a saloon, the building has seen more than its fair share of murders, suicides and accidental self-inflicted gunshot deaths since 1895. The current owner Ron Russo said that when he bought the hotel in 1990, the previous owners warned that he might not be comfortable inside the building but declined to tell him what they had seen over the years. Ron also believes that it was the ghost of an angry man that caused him to have a heart attack!

The ghost of Margaret Broadwater, a girl who "worked upstairs", took her own life by jumping out a third floor window, possibly trying to cover up the fact she was pregnant. She can be seen and heard lurking amongst the shadows of the hotel. Apparitions are very common here, especially on the third floor where guests even feel the spirits pass by as they brush against their skin or hair

Old Fairmont Hotel © Carol M. Highsmith, Public domain

On one ghost tour of the building, in a room with large windows which the hookers would wave at passersby from to try and entice them in, a guest felt something tickling her leg. Thinking it was a bug or something she tried to swat it away but there was nothing there, no bugs, no bits of cloth or anything, yet the tickling sensation continued, as if fabric was brushing back and forth against her calves. This continued until they left the room.

Numerous tv shows have been investigating Deadwood including Dead Files and Ghost Adventures, and there was even a tv series called Deadwood, which was based around the lawlessness and some of the real people and real events which happened in the town, with a healthy dose of fiction thrown in, of course!

Chapter 42

TENNESSEE

The Bell Witch

The chilling tale of the Bell Witch revolves around the Bells, a family who resided in Robertson County, Tennessee. The peaceful life of the Bell family took a dark turn in 1817, after living harmoniously in Tennessee for 13 years. Strange occurrences began to disturb their once tranquil existence as what started as subtle disturbances soon escalated into a reign of terror that plagued every room of their home.

The Bell Witch, as it came to be known, showed no mercy as it terrorised the family who became entangled with a malevolent force that haunted them relentlessly, and would become one of the most documented and evident hauntings in the annals of the paranormal.

This supernatural entity inflicted upon the family a series of unexplained noises, eerie occurrences, and physical attacks that spanned several years. Of all the Bells, the entity seemed particularly hostile towards John Bell, the patriarch, and his daughter Betsy who became the primary target of these otherworldly phenomena.

The true origins of the Bell Witch remain enigmatic, leading to various conjectures and speculations. Some accounts suggest that it embodied the spirit of Kate Batts, a neighbouring woman believed to have placed a curse on the Bell family. Another theory proposes that the Bell Witch was the vengeful apparition of a Native American wronged by John Bell. Yet another perspective posits that the entity was a manifestation of the family's own latent psychic energy.

Irrespective of its origins, the presence of the Bell Witch reverberated throughout the entire community. It was said that the entity possessed the ability to speak, engaging in conversations with members of the Bell family and their visitors. Remarkably, the Bell Witch could sing hymns and recite scripture, showing a peculiar fondness for John Bell Jr., the son of the family.

The Bell Witch's influence extended far beyond mere conversation. The Bell household became a hotbed of inexplicable sounds, with reports of knocking on doors and walls, the haunting echo of chains being dragged across the floor, and the unsettling sound of rats gnawing on bedposts. These noises often erupted suddenly and persisted throughout the night, causing great disturbance to the family's sleep.

However, the Bell Witch possessed more than auditory capabilities as witnesses recounted seeing inanimate objects moving without any physical contact. Chairs, tables, and other pieces of furniture would seemingly shift on their own accord. Some reports even suggested that the entity could be present in multiple locations simultaneously, traversing vast distances at will.

The Bell Witch's disturbances did not stop at eerie phenomena; physical assaults were also a frequent occurrence. Family members bore witness to the entity's wrath, enduring slaps, punches, pinches, and scratches. Some even claimed to have been strangled or had their hair forcefully pulled by the unseen assailant.

To add to the mystique, some witnesses reported seeing the Bell Witch take physical form. It appeared either as a large, black dog or a bird-like creature, further intensifying the air of otherworldliness surrounding the entity. Additionally, the Bell Witch was believed to possess a peculiar power over animals, capable of causing them to behave strangely or vanish altogether.

The haunting of the Bell family reached its tragic climax with the death of John Bell in 1820. The circumstances surrounding his demise fueled the legend of the Bell Witch even further. A vial containing a peculiar liquid was discovered near John Bell's deathbed, leading many to attribute his passing to the vengeful spirit. The Bell Witch had made a chilling promise to return and exact revenge on John Bell and his family, a vow that seemed eerily fulfilled with his untimely demise, while others suspected foul play involving his son or a close family friend.

The death of John Bell, of Adams, TN. Occurred December of 1820. Illustration first published in 1894.

Legend has it that Kate, a woman associated with the Bell family, was revealed to be the Bell Witch herself. In a feud with John Bell, she proclaimed her intention to return and bring doom upon him and his kin.

Subsequently, the Bell Witch disappeared, never to be seen or heard from again, except for one last appearance at John Bell's funeral where it reportedly disrupted the service by singing loud and raucous drinking songs.

The state of Tennessee has officially recognized the Bell Witch as a supernatural entity, further solidifying its status as a haunting of historical significance. The alleged burial site of the Bell Witch's remains remains concealed within an underground chamber, perpetuating the aura of mystique surrounding the legend. Curious visitors can embark on tours and ghost tours to explore the eerie remnants of the Bell Witch's presence.

Interestingly, the Bell Witch legend has influenced other works of art, drawing parallels to entities blamed for domestic abuse. The Babadook, a movie that delves into a mother's descent into madness and her terrifying treatment of her child, shares thematic similarities with the Bell Witch narrative. Furthermore, the Blair Witch Project, inspired by the Bell Witch legend, continues to chill audiences with its realistic found footage style and haunting conclusion. A testament to its long lasting appeal, the Blair Witch Project remains a must-watch for horror enthusiasts.

The legend of the Bell Witch has endured for over two centuries, captivating audiences across generations and becoming deeply ingrained in American folklore. Its enigmatic legacy continues to evoke curiosity and fascination, captivating those who dare to delve into its haunting narrative.

Chapter 43

TEXAS

The Big Thicket Ghost Light

Situated in southeast Texas, the Big Thicket sprawls across an expansive 100,000 acres, characterised by its dense woodland. This vast expanse is renowned for its remarkable array of plant and animal species, making it one of the most biodiverse regions in the entire country. Cypress swamps, hardwood forests, and piney woods harmoniously coexist within this area, constituting a range of distinct ecosystems.

Notably, the Big Thicket occupies a significant place in American history. During the era of the Civil War, it served as a sanctuary for deserters and draft dodgers, earning a reputation as a refuge for outlaws seeking to evade the law's grasp. Later, in the 20th century, the Big Thicket emerged as a pivotal hub for the conservation movement, leading to its eventual designation as a national preserve in 1974.

Embedded in the annals of this region is the captivating legend of Bragg Road. Constructed in 1934, this dirt road was built atop the remnants of a former railway that once catered to the lumber industry. The 1940s witnessed the emergence and dissemination of tales surrounding the Bragg Road Ghost Light, a peculiar luminescent phenomenon also referred to as the Light of Saratoga. It was believed to manifest itself either on or in the vicinity of the road.

Legend has it that this mysterious radiant sphere manifests exclusively during nighttime, characterised by its spectral mobility and colour-changing capabilities. Various theories have been put forth to explain the light's origin, ranging from it being the ghost of a railroad worker tragically killed during track construction to the spirit of a Native American who met a tragic end in the region.

Throughout the years, numerous individuals have claimed to have witnessed the enigmatic Bragg Road Ghost Light, transforming it into a popular attraction for tourists exploring the Big Thicket.

Pine Uplands © William L. Farr, CC BY-SA 4.0

One eyewitness account describes a sighting of the Bragg Road Ghost Light while driving along the road during the late hours of the night. According to the witness, the light manifested suddenly, exhibiting an apparent motion. The witness also reported experiencing an unsettling sensation, and the light vanished as they approached it.

Another testimony entails an encounter with the Bragg Road Ghost Light while walking along the road after sunset. As relayed by the witness, the light seemed to trail their footsteps, continuously shifting its hues. The witness further described hearing peculiar sounds and feeling an inexplicable cold draft, despite the warm night air.

A third individual reported spotting the Bragg Road Ghost Light while partaking in a guided tour of the Big Thicket. The tour guide drew attention to the light and recounted the legend surrounding it. The witness attested to observing the light manoeuvring and altering its colours, remaining perplexed as to its underlying cause.

One intriguing question that arises is whether this luminous phenomenon is in any way connected to sightings of a creature resembling Bigfoot, colloquially referred to as the 'wild man of the Big Thicket.'

In the early 1960s, a group of teenagers claimed to have encountered a large, hairy entity near Bragg Road. According to their description, the creature boasted a humanoid shape, completely enveloped in dark hair. They observed it ambulating on two legs, towering over ordinary humans in terms of height.

During the 1970s, a party of hunters reported a sighting of a massive, ape-like being covered in hair, standing at a staggering height of over 7 feet. The creature appeared to be observing them from a distance, instilling such fright that they promptly retreated from the area.

Pursuit of the Paranormal

In the 1990s, a man recounted an experience involving the sighting of a large, ape-like creature in the vicinity of the Village Creek area within the Big Thicket. According to the witness, the creature possessed lengthy arms, adorned in dark hair, and was situated near a creek as if quenching its thirst.

In 2012, a man purportedly captured a video depicting a Bigfoot-like creature within the confines of the Big Thicket. The footage exhibits a towering, hairy entity traversing the forest; nevertheless, the quality remains blurred and inconclusive. While the individual behind the recording insists it constitutes a genuine Bigfoot sighting, sceptics posit the possibility of a hoax or misidentification of an animal.

In 2017, a woman offered her own testimony of encountering a Bigfoot-like creature near the Pine Island Bayou area of the Big Thicket. She recollected the creature standing at the roadside, engrossed in devouring something. Its broad shoulders and hair-covered physique added to her description.

Despite concerted efforts to elucidate the nature of the Bragg Road Ghost Light, it persists as an enduring enigma. Whether attributable to a natural phenomenon or a genuine otherworldly manifestation, the legend of the Bragg Road Ghost Light, coupled with multiple accounts of purported Bigfoot encounters, continues to captivate and enthral visitors to the Big Thicket. These tales have ingrained themselves within the cultural heritage and folklore of the region, cementing their significance.

Paranormal United States

Chapter 44

UTAH

The Skinwalkers

Found deep within the vast expanse of Utah lies the infamous Skinwalker Ranch, a place shrouded in enigmatic tales and unexplained phenomena. Over time, this ranch has gained notoriety due to a myriad of reports detailing strange and perplexing occurrences. Witness accounts have revealed sightings of unidentified flying objects, elusive cryptids, and peculiar creatures roaming the grounds. Bizarre incidents such as poltergeist activity, inexplicable cattle mutilations, and mysterious lights illuminating the sky have further intensified the mystique surrounding this enigmatic location. Despite numerous investigations, official and unofficial alike, the riddles of Skinwalker Ranch persist, refusing to be unravelled.

Covering approximately 480 acres of land, Skinwalker Ranch rests in the heart of the Uintah Basin—a region inhabited by Native American tribes for countless generations and often associated with extraordinary happenings. The ranch was originally owned by a family who reported seeing strange lights and creatures on the property, leading to their decision to sell it to a group of investors in 1996.

These investors were led by Robert Bigelow who, through his company Bigelow Aerospace, established the National Institute for Discovery Science (NIDS). The purpose of NIDS was to conduct scientific research into areas such as UFOs, paranormal phenomena, and other unexplained events.

Under Bigelow's ownership, NIDS researchers conducted extensive investigations at Skinwalker Ranch, employing various scientific instruments and methods to document and analyse the reported phenomena. The research team claimed to have witnessed and recorded unusual events, including sightings of unidentified flying objects, strange creatures, crop circles, and poltergeist-like activities.

Among the most remarkable incidents reported on the ranch is the presence of a creature known as the Skinwalker. Rooted in Navajo folklore, the Skinwalker is depicted as a malevolent witch or sorcerer capable of shape-shifting into various animal forms. Legend has it that this formidable being possesses the power to assume any desired form and employs its abilities to inflict harm or manipulate others.

According to Navajo beliefs, encountering a Skinwalker serves as an omen of imminent danger or death. Furthermore, it is believed that Skinwalkers acquire their powers through a ritual that necessitates the killing of a close family member. Passed down through generations, the legend of the Skinwalker holds great significance within Navajo culture and traditions.

Multiple reports of Skinwalker sightings have surfaced, with witnesses describing a large, dark figure that moves with uncanny agility and grace, defying natural limitations.

Beyond the tale of the Skinwalker, a plethora of Native American stories and legends are intertwined with the region surrounding Skinwalker Ranch. These accounts encompass tales of potent spirits, sacred sites, and supernatural occurrences. Passed down through the ages, these narratives play a pivotal role in the spiritual and cultural traditions of the Native American tribes residing in the area.

Modern reports from the ranch include encounters with impervious wolves, seemingly immune to bullets, as well as sightings of hairless dogs or hyena-like creatures of significant proportions. Witnesses have also described sightings of winged beings reminiscent of pterodactyls, along with UFO sightings and unexplained lights that dot the sky.

Access to Skinwalker Ranch is very restricted
Skinwalker Ranch © Paul from USA, CC BY-SA 2.0

One of the most unsettling aspects of the mysterious events at Skinwalker Ranch is the recurring phenomenon of cattle mutilations. Numerous instances have been documented where cattle have been discovered with missing tongues, genitals, and peculiar incisions and puncture wounds. Some of these unfortunate animals have even been found with surgically precise organ removals.

These grotesque mutilations remain unexplained, with some researchers postulating that they may be the work of extraterrestrial or interdimensional entities.

Despite extensive investigations, conclusive explanations for the bizarre happenings at Skinwalker Ranch elude us. Some propose a connection to natural geological or atmospheric phenomena, such as seismic activity or the occurrence of ball lightning. Others theorise that the ranch might serve as a portal to alternate dimensions or or that it is the site of secret government experiments

In recent years, Skinwalker Ranch has undergone a resurgence of interest, with Brandon Fugal, a Utah-based businessman assuming ownership and facilitating scientific research on the property. Investing substantial sums of money, Fugal has upgraded the premises and implemented cutting-edge technology to aid in the investigation of these extraordinary occurrences. The ranch has also become the subject of a documentary series aired on the History Channel called 'The Secret of Skinwalker Ranch.' boasting multiple seasons of investigations at the location.

While the mysteries encircling the perplexing events at Skinwalker Ranch may forever evade resolution, one thing remains clear—the area boasts a rich and intricate history intricately woven into the legends and traditions of the Native American peoples who have called it home for countless millennia.

Chapter 45

VERMONT

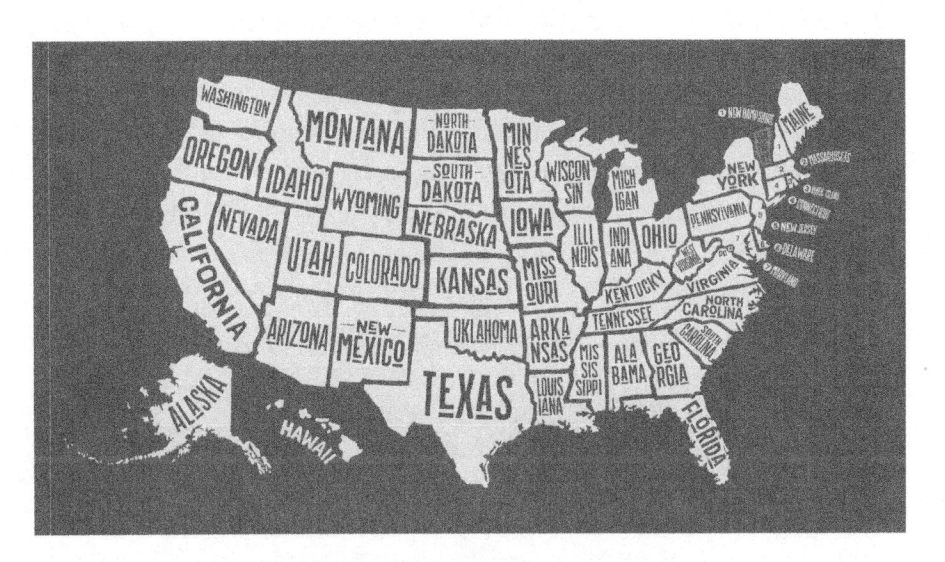

The Bennington Triangle

Nestled in the captivating landscape of southwestern Vermont lies the enigmatic Bennington Triangle, an area shrouded in mystery due to numerous unexplained phenomena and a string of perplexing disappearances. The boundaries of this bewitching region encompass the towns of Bennington, Woodford, Shaftsbury, and Somerset, forming an eerie and alluring triangle of intrigue.

One of the most renowned incidents associated with the Bennington Triangle took place in 1945 when a skilled outdoorsman named Middie Rivers vanished while hunting in the area. Despite exhaustive search efforts, Rivers seemed to have vanished without a trace, save for a lone rifle cartridge discovered in a nearby stream, serving as a haunting reminder of his inexplicable disappearance.

Another puzzling occurrence unfolded on December 1, 1946, when 18-year-old Paula Jean Welden set out on a hike along the Long

Trail. Welden, a sophomore at Bennington College, was last seen by several witnesses, including Ernest Whitman, an employee of the Bennington Banner who had given her directions. Surprisingly, despite the chilly 50 °F weather, Welden embarked on her hike without wearing a jacket. As she ventured into the trail, an elderly couple reported sighting her about 100 yards ahead. However, when the couple reached the same corner where Welden had turned, she had mysteriously vanished into thin air. Despite extensive search operations, no trace of Welden was ever uncovered, leaving behind an eerie void that inspired Shirley Jackson's haunting 1951 novel, Hangsaman.

Bennington © King of Hearts, CC BY-SA 4.0

Three years later, on the exact same date of December 1, 1949, another peculiar disappearance unfolded within the Bennington Triangle. James E. Tedford, a veteran and resident of the Bennington Soldiers' Home, inexplicably vanished under puzzling circumstances. Tedford had been visiting his relatives in St. Albans and was last seen boarding a local bus. Witnesses on the bus confirmed his presence until the final stop before Bennington. Astonishingly, between that last stop and the bus's arrival in

Bennington, Tedford disappeared without a trace. When the bus reached its destination, his belongings remained undisturbed in the luggage rack, and an open bus timetable rested on his vacant seat. While some speculate that Tedford vanished into the ether, there exists a perplexing gap between the last confirmed sighting of him and his reported disappearance a week later.

In another chilling incident, eight-year-old Paul Jepson vanished on October 12, 1950, while accompanying his mother in a truck. Jepson's mother briefly left him unattended to feed some pigs, but upon her return, her son had inexplicably vanished. Despite the striking visibility of his bright red jacket, no trace of the young boy was ever found, despite extensive search efforts. Curiously, one tale suggests that bloodhounds utilised in the search tracked Jepson to a nearby highway, where Paula Jean Welden had vanished four years earlier, a haunting coincidence that deepens the mystery surrounding the Bennington Triangle.

Somerset Reservoir © Jessamyn, Public domain

On October 28, 1950, a perplexing event unfolded involving 53-year-old Frieda Langer and her cousin Herbert Elsner. The pair embarked on a hike after departing from their family campsite near the Somerset Reservoir. While traversing their journey, Langer stumbled into a stream and instructed Elsner to wait while she returned to the campsite to change her soaked attire and catch up. However, Langer never returned, and upon Elsner's arrival at the campsite, he discovered her absence. Despite extensive search efforts involving aircraft, helicopters, and up to 300 searchers, no trace of Langer was ever unearthed, leaving her disappearance as an enduring enigma within the Bennington Triangle.

Beyond the perplexing vanishings, reports of peculiar creatures have permeated the lore of the Bennington Triangle. The most notorious is the "Bennington Monster" or "Bennington Beast," a cryptid alleged to roam the area. Descriptions of this creature vary, with witnesses commonly attributing its appearance to a large, hairy animal with sharp teeth and glowing eyes. Some liken it to a fusion of a bear and a cat, while others draw parallels to the infamous Bigfoot or Sasquatch.

The first documented sighting of the Bennington Monster dates back to the 19th century, and sporadic reports of its existence have persisted over time. In 1973, a group of four hunters claimed a harrowing encounter with the creature in the Glastenbury Wilderness area of Vermont. According to their harrowing account, the beast stood at an imposing seven feet tall, possessed a muscular build, and had piercing red eyes and razor-sharp teeth. Despite the hunters firing multiple shots at the creature, it inexplicably vanished into the dense woodland, seemingly impervious to harm.

Sceptics contend that the Bennington Monster may be misidentifications of known animals, such as bears, while believers argue for the existence of an undiscovered or prehistoric species. There are even speculations that the creature possesses supernatural attributes, potentially being a shape-shifter or a malevolent entity from the realm of the occult.

In addition to the enigmatic disappearances and sightings of strange creatures, the Bennington Triangle has also become a hotbed for UFO encounters and unexplained lights, including the presence of glowing orbs witnessed throughout the years. Consequently, the allure of the Bennington Triangle continues to beckon paranormal enthusiasts and inquisitive travellers, offering an intriguing blend of natural beauty and unexplained phenomena.

Chapter 46

VIRGINIA

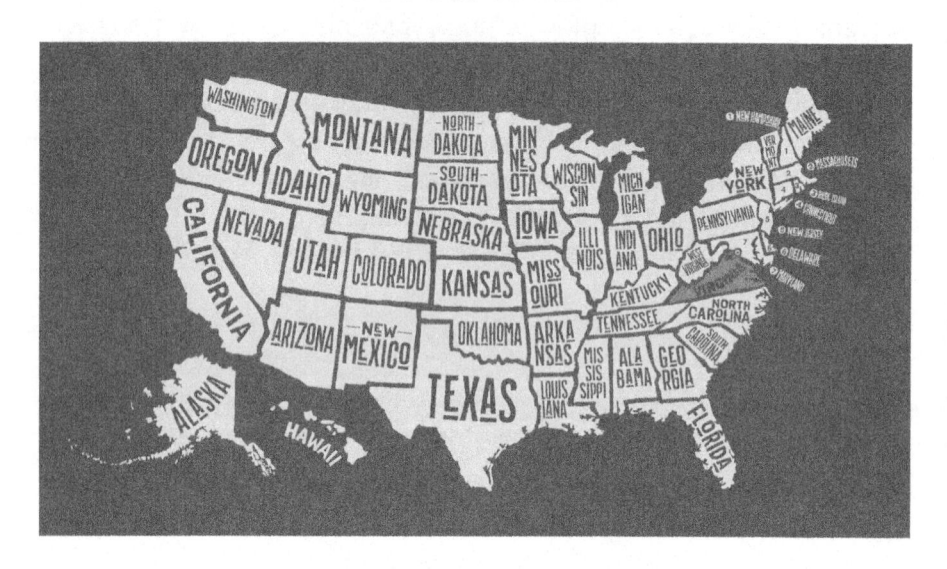

The Study of Past Lives

The University of Virginia School of Medicine, situated in Charlottesville, Virginia, holds a distinguished status as one of the oldest medical schools in the United States, having been established by Thomas Jefferson in 1819. The University's Division of Perceptual Studies is not your average academic department. Founded in 1967, this enigmatic institution delves into the mysteries of paranormal phenomena and investigates the possibility of personality surviving beyond death.

Dr. Ian Stevenson, a renowned psychiatrist and researcher affiliated with the University, gained prominence through his extensive investigation into instances where children claimed to possess memories of past lives. Throughout his illustrious career, Dr. Stevenson interviewed numerous children and their families, meticulously documenting their detailed accounts of previous existences.

Dr. Stevenson's research predominantly concentrated on cases worldwide, with a special focus on India, a country deeply rooted in the belief of reincarnation. His findings revealed that many of the children he studied were capable of providing specific information concerning their alleged past selves, including names, locations, and events. Remarkably, some of these children exhibited birthmarks or scars that directly corresponded to injuries sustained by their past incarnations.

Inset: Dr Ian Stevenson © 2007 by the Rector and Visitors of the University of Virginia

One of the most compelling cases highlighting past life memories is that of Shanti Devi. Born in Delhi, India during the 1930s, Shanti began recounting details of a previous life at an early age. At four years old, she confided in her parents that her true home lay in Mathura, a city located 145 km away from Delhi, where her husband purportedly resided.

Despite her parents' initial scepticism, Shanti persistently maintained her claim of a previous life in Mathura. At the age of six, she even ran away from home in an attempt to reach Mathura. Furthermore, while attending school, Shanti professed to being married and narrated the story of her demise, which occurred ten days after giving birth.

Shanti's teacher and headmaster were astounded when they interviewed her and she spoke fluently in the Mathura dialect while revealing the name of her merchant husband, "Kedar Nath." Intrigued by this revelation, the headmaster decided to investigate further and discovered a merchant in Mathura named Kedar Nath. Remarkably, Kedar Nath had lost his wife, Lugdi Devi, nine years prior, just ten days after she had given birth to a son.

Dr. Stevenson conducted an investigation into the case and interviewed Shanti in 1986. However, an earlier investigation commissioned by Mahatma Gandhi had already concluded that Shanti was the reincarnation of Lugdi Devi.

Another remarkable case examined by Dr. Stevenson was that of James Leininger, a young boy from Louisiana. James began experiencing vivid nightmares of being a World War II pilot when he was just two years old. Startled, he would wake up crying out, "Airplane crash, plane on fire, little man can't get out!" When James' parents inquired about these distressing dreams, he provided intricate details about the life of a man named James Huston Jr., who had perished during World War II.

Dr. Stevenson delved into James Leininger's claims and discovered that many of the details he had provided about James Huston Jr.'s life were remarkably accurate. James correctly identified the type of aircraft that Huston Jr. had flown and even named the aircraft carrier on which he had been stationed. Furthermore, James accurately recalled the names of some of Huston Jr.'s comrades.

Dr. Stevenson's investigation unearthed additional evidence corroborating James Leininger's assertions. He verified the existence of James Huston Jr., who had indeed lost his life in the Pacific during World War II. Moreover, some of the individuals who had served alongside Huston Jr. confirmed that James Leininger accurately identified them by name.

The media extensively covered this case, and James's parents eventually authored a best-selling book detailing their investigation. Initially, their intention was to disprove their son's claims due to their devout Christian beliefs, which made them uncomfortable with the notion of reincarnation.

Intriguingly, studies on reincarnation have uncovered over 2,500 cases where children have shared stories about past lives. The innocence and honesty of these young individuals make their accounts particularly compelling evidence. Researchers endeavour to explore the depths of these stories, seeking insights into the nature of consciousness and the potential continuity of life beyond death.

The University of Virginia's Division of Perceptual Studies and Dr. Stevenson's work is a beacon of scientific inquiry into the realms of the paranormal and life after death. With their groundbreaking research and compelling evidence, they challenge conventional notions and encourage us to explore the uncharted territories of human consciousness. While some interpret it as evidence supporting reincarnation and the continuity of consciousness beyond death, others perceive it as mere coincidence or the consequence of suggestion and cultural beliefs. Regardless of one's stance, the cases examined by Dr. Stevenson continue to captivate and provoke thought, representing a fascinating and intriguing area of study.

Chapter 47

WASHINGTON

Fort Worden

Washington State is known for its breathtaking natural beauty and rich history, but it is also home to one of the most haunted places in the region - Fort Worden campground. Situated on the Olympic Peninsula in Port Townsend, Washington, the fort holds a rich history as a significant military installation. Dating back to the late 1800s, it was established as part of the United States' coastal defence system, guarding the entrance to Puget Sound from potential enemy threats. Throughout the 20th century, the fort served as a pivotal military site, playing a vital role in safeguarding the Pacific Northwest and the West Coast of the United States during both World Wars.

Originally known as the Artillery District of Puget Sound, Fort Worden underwent construction during the late 1800s to fortify the region against foreign invasion. Its strategic importance was highlighted during World War I and World War II, as it served as a shield protecting the Pacific Northwest and the entire West Coast from potential adversaries.

Following World War II, the military decommissioned Fort Worden, transferring its ownership to the state of Washington. Over the years, the base witnessed various incidents and transformations, including the establishment of a jail for enlisted personnel and its later conversion into a treatment facility for troubled youth. Adding to the eerie atmosphere is an on-site military cemetery, where the spirits of past soldiers are believed to linger

Since then, it has evolved into a popular destination, drawing tourists and locals alike with its diverse recreational and educational offerings. Within the fort's premises, visitors can find a conference centre, a campground, and an array of recreational facilities, including scenic hiking and biking trails, picturesque beaches, and inviting picnic areas.

Among the notable landmarks at Fort Worden is the renowned Point Wilson Lighthouse, constructed in 1914. Serving as a guiding beacon for ships navigating the waters of Puget Sound, this majestic lighthouse continues to operate today, captivating the attention of visitors who flock to the fort.

Fort Worden c.1923 © University of Washington, Public domain

Pursuit of the Paranormal

In addition to its historical significance and natural allure, Fort Worden has garnered a reputation for being haunted, with numerous ghost stories and paranormal investigations surrounding its premises. Locals and visitors have reported encounters with several apparitions, adding an extra layer of intrigue to the fort's mystique.

One of the most famous ghostly figures said to roam Fort Worden is a soldier frequently spotted on the parade ground. Witnesses describe him as donning a uniform reminiscent of the early 1900s, marching purposefully with an air of determination. Encounterers of this spectral soldier often report an unsettling sense of unease or foreboding in his presence.

Another commonly reported ghost is a woman believed to haunt the vicinity of Building 298, formerly a military hospital and morgue, which itself holds a particular air of unease due to its preserved bloodletting table. However, it has garnered notoriety for sightings of a mysterious woman appearing in a second-story window every night at approximately 10:30 p.m., clutching a lit candle. Legend has it that she was a nurse serving during World War II, meeting an untimely demise under mysterious circumstances within the hospital's confines. Visitors recount feeling a chilling presence, hearing unexplained sounds, and even witnessing the ethereal manifestation of a woman adorned in a nurse's uniform.

Megan Claflin, spokesperson for the public-development authority overseeing Fort Worden's various entities, acknowledges that reports of peculiar sightings and inexplicable sounds have persisted for more than a century among both residents and visitors.

Furthermore, the guardhouse, once a detention centre for soldiers who violated military regulations, is also said to be a site of spectral activity. Visitors have attested to hearing phantom footsteps and disembodied voices within the empty building, accompanied by an uncanny sensation of being observed or touched by unseen forces, as well as the smell of burning rubber or hot sulphur.

A Seattle paranormal investigator even managed to capture an apparition dressed in purple clothing in a photograph taken at the guard house, adding visual evidence to the other many first-hand reports.

Fort Worden © Mamabrooking, CC BY-SA 3.0

One area within the guard house that stands out for its eerie ambiance is the dark basement. Although small in size, this dimly lit space is said to be the home of a former guard who tragically ended his own life with a pistol and who can still be felt and seen in this basement. His lingering spirit serves as a chilling reminder of the emotional weight and history embedded within the walls of Fort Worden.

Hikers and campers recount eerie moans resonating through the dim corridors of the barracks on overcast days. As the sun descends, flickering lights mysteriously illuminate certain buildings devoid of electrical power.

Fort Worden, with its captivating history, natural beauty, and tales of the supernatural, continues to captivate the imagination of those who venture within its storied walls. Whether you are a believer in the paranormal or a sceptic, the chilling encounters reported by countless visitors cannot be easily dismissed.

Paranormal United States

Chapter 48

WEST VIRGINIA

The Haunted Theme Park

In the heart of West Virginia lies a forgotten gem, Lake Shawnee Amusement Park, situated in Mercer County. This former family-friendly attraction holds a captivating history filled with both joy and tragedy. Established in 1926, the park entertained visitors for four decades before succumbing to financial hardships and closing its gates in 1966. Among its attractions were a thrilling Ferris wheel, an exhilarating roller coaster, a delightful swing ride, and a sprawling swimming pool that provided respite from the summer heat.

However, the site's past is shrouded in darkness and misfortune. Prior to the park's construction, the land held an ancient secret—a Native American burial ground, with mass graves being stumbled upon by archeologists, rumoured to be the final resting place for up to 3000 souls. In 1783, a family settled on the land, and their children formed bonds with the Native American children of a neighbouring tribe. Tragically, according to legend, the three young settlers met their untimely demise at the hands of the Native Americans. Disturbing accounts suggest that the children were scalped, their lifeless bodies left as a chilling warning to other settlers.

Throughout the amusement park's existence, a series of tragic events unfolded, perpetuating the sense of sorrow that seemed to haunt the grounds. Two children lost their lives to the park's pool, their innocent laughter silenced forever. The first incident involved a young boy, whose mother left him under the watchful eyes of the open-air pool attendants, only to return and find him inexplicably missing. Despite an exhaustive search throughout the park, the boy's lifeless body was tragically discovered floating in the pool. Years later, an eleven-year-old boy met a similar fate, his arm ensnared by a pool drain, leading to his untimely demise.

In a macabre twist of fate, tragedy struck the park once more in 1966. During a routine delivery, a lorry inadvertently reversed into the path of the towering swing ride. As fate would have it, a young girl occupied one of the swings, and her life was abruptly ended when her seat collided with the back of the vehicle. This heartbreaking incident served as the catalyst for the park's ultimate closure out of respect for the grieving families.

Abandoned Swings © Forsaken Fotos Maryland, CC BY 2.0

The accumulation of such tragic events, coupled with whispered tales of additional deaths and accidents within the park, has nurtured a belief among many that Lake Shawnee Amusement Park is a place plagued by paranormal activity. Visitors have shared spine-chilling accounts of encountering ghostly apparitions, hearing inexplicable noises and voices, and experiencing otherworldly phenomena. The park has become a magnet for paranormal investigators and has garnered attention through numerous appearances on television shows and documentaries dedicated to exploring haunted locations and restless spirits.

Witnesses often recount sightings of a spectral figure closely resembling one of the young boys who perished in the pool. This ghostly manifestation is frequently observed near the very pool where the tragedy occurred, with some visitors even reporting hearing the faint echoes of giggles or the child calling out for his parents. Another apparition that captivates visitors is that of a young girl, her ethereal form wandering near the swing ride or occasionally occupying the seat adorned with a pink ribbon, symbolising her tragic fate.

Adding to the supernatural tapestry of Lake Shawnee Amusement Park is the haunting presence of a Native American warrior. Draped in traditional attire and brandishing a tomahawk, this spectral figure roams the grounds - a not entirely surprising phenomenon considering the deep-rooted Native American history associated with the site.

In 1985, Gaylord White acquired the land with aspirations of resurrecting the theme park. However, his plans were forever halted when an archaeological dig unearthed the remains of thirteen individuals, predominantly children. This grim discovery further underscored the sombre history and unsettling aura surrounding the park.

Lake Shawnee Amusement Park © Forsaken Fotos Maryland, CC BY 2.0

Despite its dark past, Lake Shawnee Amusement Park remains an alluring destination for visitors drawn to its eerie history. Many guests pay their respects by leaving toys and dolls as offerings to the innocent children who tragically lost their lives within its boundaries. The park stands as a poignant reminder of the delicate balance between joy and sorrow, and the lingering echoes of the past that can permeate our present-day experiences.

Chapter 49

WISCONSIN

The Devils Lake

Nestled within the picturesque Baraboo Range of south-central Wisconsin, Devil's Lake State Park stands as a beloved destination for nature enthusiasts and adventure seekers alike. This enchanting park derives its name from the sprawling Devil's Lake, a magnificent 360-acre body of water that took shape more than 12,000 years ago, sculpted by the mighty hands of ancient glaciers.

The lake's allure lies not only in its serene waters but also in the majestic quartzite bluffs that encircle it, forming an awe-inspiring backdrop of natural splendour. The towering bluffs have become a magnet for rock climbers and hikers, calling on them to embark on thrilling adventures. With over 29 miles of trails meandering through the park, visitors can choose from a range of hiking options, from leisurely strolls along tranquil paths to invigorating treks. It comes as no surprise that this natural haven attracts approximately 1.5 million visitors each year, drawn to its awe-inspiring beauty and the mystique that has surrounded it since its discovery.

Water enthusiasts flock to Devil's Lake, where a plethora of aquatic activities await their eager participation. Swimming, fishing, boating—these are but a few of the pastimes that can be enjoyed within the park's pristine waters. Two sandy beaches, nestled within the park's boundaries, offer sun-soaked havens for visitors to bask in the warmth of the sun and indulge in the joys of swimming.

Devil's Lake State Park, Wisconsin © http://www.goodfreephotos.com

Beyond its natural wonders, Devil's Lake State Park boasts a rich cultural history that adds a layer of intrigue to its already captivating allure. In ancient times, the Ho-Chunk Native American tribe called this land home, infusing the area with their vibrant presence. Today, remnants of this storied past can be found in the park's archaeological sites, serving as a testament to the enduring legacy of these indigenous people. Moreover, the park proudly houses several historic structures, including a 19th-century chapel and a Civilian Conservation Corps (CCC) camp, each steeped in the essence of a bygone era.

Adding to the park's mystique are the various legends and folklore surrounding Devil's Lake. Known as "Ta-wa-cun-chuk-dah" in the Winnebago language, meaning "Sacred Lake," the lake has inspired a myriad of translations: Holy Lake, Mystery Lake, Spirit Lake, Wild Beauty Lake, and Bad Spirit Lake. Native American tales have woven a tapestry of wonder, recounting the lake's origin and the occurrence of supernatural phenomena.

One legend speaks of a titanic clash between colossal thunderbirds, known as Wakhakeera, and water monsters called Wakunja, who resided deep within the lake's cavernous depths. In this epic struggle, thunderbolts rained down from the sky as the birds soared overhead, while the water monsters retaliated with mighty rock formations and towering water spouts.

Another captivating tale involves a fearsome green dragon that claimed the heart of the lake as its dominion. With seven heads and a body impervious to arrows, this omnipotent creature was believed to be the creator of the lake. It demanded regular offerings, including the yearly sacrifice of a fair maiden, according to the beliefs of the indigenous people.

Though these legends and folklore tantalise the imagination, offering glimpses into a world of fantasy, the experiences of many visitors to Devil's Lake State Park paint a more mysterious picture. Reports of encounters with enigmatic lake monsters surface, describing sightings of a colossal serpentine beast and an octopus-like creature.

Moreover, eerie apparitions and elusive shadows are said to roam the park, particularly near the historic structures like the chapel and CCC camp. Some visitors claim to have heard disembodied voices or experienced the haunting echo of footsteps in these areas.

Curious phenomena have also been documented, such as unexplained equipment malfunctions and uncharacteristic cold spots that send shivers down the spine. A sense of unease and the uncanny feeling of being watched have been reported by individuals exploring certain sections of the park.

Moving beyond the lakes, on the nearby Highway 12 which runs alongside the Devils Lake, there are reports abound of a phantom hitchhiker who mysteriously vanishes and reappears further down the road, leaving bewildered witnesses in its wake. Adding to the highway's supernatural aura, a 1954 issue of Fate magazine documents spine-chilling sightings of ghostly elephants wandering along its path. These ghostly apparitions, said to have haunted the streets of Baraboo, Wisconsin, have been linked to nighttime crashes and eerie creaking sounds.

Could this photo be evidence of a ghostly elephant or even a hairless mammoth, raising questions about the unknown creatures that may roam the wilderness?

Ghost Elephant © Derrick A. Mayoleth / Skillet Creek Media

Devil's Lake State Park captures the essence of natural beauty intertwined with captivating legends, and unexplained supernatural occurrences. From its majestic bluffs to the tranquil waters of the lake, this enchanting destination invites visitors to immerse themselves in a realm where folklore meets breathtaking scenery.

Chapter 50

WYOMING

Spirits of Fort Laramie

Fort Laramie, located along the banks of the Laramie River in Goshen County, Wyoming, was an important military outpost and trading centre during the 19th century. During its operation, many soldiers, traders, and Native Americans passed through the fort, and it's said that some of their spirits may still linger there.

During its time as a military outpost, Fort Laramie was often involved in battles with Native American tribes, particularly during the mid-19th century when tensions between settlers and Native Americans were high. It's estimated that several dozen soldiers were killed in battles around the fort during this time.

Additionally, the fort was also a place where diseases like cholera and smallpox were common, and many people may have died from these illnesses while staying at the fort.

Pursuit of the Paranormal

It's likely that several dozen or even hundreds of people may have died at Fort Laramie during its time as a military outpost and trading centre. There have been numerous reports of paranormal activity at Fort Laramie over the years, with some people claiming to have seen ghostly figures and heard strange noises.

This spirit of The Lady in Green is one of the most well-known spirits at Fort Laramie, and her ghost has been reportedly seen by numerous people over the years. The Lady in Green is the ghost of a young woman who visited the site when it was known as Fort John, an American Fur Company trading post

An accomplished equestrian, the lady, who was the daughter of the agent in charge of the trading post at the time, slipped away one night riding a big black horse. She was soon spotted and two men quickly chased after, asking her to stop. She ignored them and managed to get away, never to return. What happened to her remains a mystery but it is her ghost which is said to appear every seven years on a trail running alongside the fort.

The Lady in Green is typically described as a beautiful woman dressed in a flowing green dress, with long brown hair tucked up beneath a veiled hat and a sad expression on her face. She is said to wander the grounds of the fort, sometimes appearing suddenly before disappearing again just as quickly. Some people who have seen her have reported feeling a cold breeze or a sudden drop in temperature, as if the ghostly presence has brought a chill to the air.

This ghost known as The Cavalry Officer is said to be a soldier who died while stationed at Fort Laramie. There are different versions of the story of the Cavalry Officer's death. Some accounts claim that he was killed in battle during an attack by Native American warriors. Other stories suggest that he died of illness or in an accident while on duty.

The ghost of the Cavalry Officer is said to be a full-bodied apparition, often seen dressed in the uniform of a cavalry soldier from the 19th century. He is typically described as tall and lean, with a serious expression on his face. Witnesses who have seen the Cavalry Officer's ghost report that he often appears suddenly and then disappears just as quickly, as if he is still patrolling the grounds of the fort.

Old Bedlam - in Fort Laramie National Historic Site, Wyoming
© Paul Hermans

In addition to sightings of the Cavalry Officer's ghost, some people have reported hearing the sounds of hooves and jingling spurs, as if a horse and rider are passing by. Others have reported hearing the sound of military drums or bugles in the distance, as if the fort's former inhabitants are still carrying out their duties.

Other commonly reported spirits include a young man in a raincoat who seems to be talking to somebody although there's nobody there; An angry-looking surgeon wearing a blood-covered uniform; and at the nearby Deer Creek, a headless man has been seen throwing rocks into the water.

Stories and rumours about supernatural activity have circulated for many years. However, there are documented reports of strange occurrences and ghostly sightings at the fort dating back to the early 20th century.

One of the earliest written accounts of paranormal activity at Fort Laramie was published in the "Laramie Boomerang" newspaper on February 19, 1920. The article described a group of soldiers who had been stationed at the fort in the late 1800s and claimed to have seen ghostly apparitions during their time there.

Since then, many other accounts of ghostly sightings and strange occurrences at Fort Laramie have been reported by visitors, staff, and paranormal investigators. These stories have helped to cement the fort's reputation as one of the most haunted places in the American West.

Fort Laramie NHS-Gate © Chris Light at English Wikipedia, CC BY-SA 3.0

With Thanks

We hope that you have enjoyed this journey around the Paranormal United States, and trust that we have given you enough taste of each of these weird and unusual stories that you are left wanting to find out more!

We would love to hear your feedback so please get in touch with us on our website

www.pursuitoftheparanormal.co.uk

Or email us at

podcast@pursuitoftheparanormal.co.uk

If you are feeling really generous, a rating or review of the book on Amazon really goes a long way and we will also shout you out on a future episode of the podcast!

If you haven't listened to the podcast before, you can find us on most podcast platforms, just search for
Pursuit of the Paranormal

Pursuit of the Paranormal

About the Authors

Ash Ellis

After a UFO sighting at the age of 10, Manchester-based Ash has since spent a lifetime trying to figure out what he saw, ultimately leading to his founding of UFOIdentified.co.uk and the UKs biggest database of current-day UFO sightings. After a ghostly encounter in a pub in 2018 this interest spread to other areas of the paranormal and Ash now has a keen interest in anything considered out of the ordinary and investigates both UFO sightings and other paranormal reports, even including alleged bigfoot sightings in the UK.

Greg Thomlinson

As a child, Greg grew up in the 80's watching programmes like Tomorrow's World and especially, Arthur C Clarke's Mysterious World where he learnt about high strangeness and the paranormal. It was on this programme that Greg 1st heard about poltergeists and spontaneous human combustion which started his fascination in everything weird. After joining a local paranormal research group near Oxford, he has now dedicated many years to understanding things that are considered out of the ordinary.

Pursuit of the Paranormal

Attributions

Chapter 1
Pickens Courthouse © Brian Collins www.atomicpix.com
Faceinthewindow © Brian Collins www.atomicpix.com
Chapter 2
"Matanuska Glacier, Alaska" by Paxson Woelber is licensed under CC BY 2.0
Chapter 3
"Yuma Territorial Prison State Historic Park, Yuma, Arizona (50)" by Ken Lund is licensed under CC BY-SA 2.0.
"Yuma Territorial Prison State Historic Park, Yuma, Arizona (32)" by Ken Lund is licensed under CC BY-SA 2.0.
Chapter 4
Fouke Monster by Romana Klee is licensed under CC BY-SA 2.0
Chapter 5
Hugh Hefner's Mansion © Carol M. Highsmith, Public domain
Holly Madison derivative work © Luke Ford, lukeford.net, CC BY-SA 2.5
Chapter 6
Blucifer at the Denver International Airport © Mike Sinko Photography by CC BY-SA 2.0
Gargoyle Statue © Bigmacthealmanac, CC BY-SA 4.0
Chapter 7
Norwich Hospital District Admin Building © CLK Hatcher, CC BY-SA 2.0
Abandoned Theatre © Abandoned America www.abandonedamerica.us
Chapter 8
Maggie's Bridge © Chesapeake Ghosts https://chesapeakeghosts.com
"Cannonball House" by jjmusgrove is licensed under CC BY 2.0
Chapter 9
Skunk Ape 2019 © Dave Shealy
"Skunk Ape Cast Expedition Bigfoot The Sasquatch Museum Blue Ridge Georgia" by amanderson2 is licensed under CC BY-SA 2.0
Chapter 10
Lake Lanier July 2018 © Thomson200, CC0
Chapter 11
Pali Road c1883 and 1905 © Gabriel Bertram Bellinghausen, Public domain
Pali Lookout © InSapphoWeTrust CC BY-SA 2.0
Chapter 12
PocatelloHigh © Beantwo, CC BY-SA 3.0

Pursuit of the Paranormal

Chapter 13
Mineral Springs Hotel, Alton IL © Great Rivers & Routes Tourism www.riversandroutes.com
Alton Military Prison. Unknown author, Public domain

Chapter 14
Crown Hill Cemetery Gateway Arches © Tom Woodward, CC BY-SA 2.0
Slippery Noodle Inn © Sarah Stierch CC BY 4.0

Chapter 15
"Josiah B. and Sara Moore House - Villisca" by Jason McLaren is licensed under CC BY-SA 4.0
Chicago News © The day book, Public domain

Chapter 16
Sallie House © Visit Atchison, https://visitatchison.com

Chapter 17
"Hopkinsville goblin" by Tim Bertelink is licensed under CC BY-SA 4.0.

Chapter 18
Delphine LaLaurie © Unknown author, Public domain
LaLaurie Mansion © APK, CC BY-SA 4.0

Chapter 19
FortKnoxtoBucksport © Leonard G.CC SA 1.0
Buck's Tomb © DrStew82, CC BY-SA 4.0

Chapter 20
Chesapeake and Ohio Canal National Historical Park © National Park Service Digital Image Archives, Public domain
Chesapeake and Ohio Canal 1900-1928 © E.B. Thompson, Public domain

Chapter 21
USS Salem Museum © Sswonk, Public domain
USS Salem underway in the Mediterranean Sea on 16 June 1952 © Naval History & Heritage Command, Public domain

Chapter 22
Paulding Light © Flivver 99 at English Wikipedia, CC BY 3.0
Pauldinglight © https://www.ontonagonmi.com

Chapter 23
Colonial Hall and Masonic Lodge No 30 © McGhiever, CC BY-SA 3.0
Jackson Hotel © McGhiever, CC BY-SA 3.0

Chapter 24
King's Tavern © Ralph Clynne, Public domain
Natchez MS 1850's © Henry Lewis, Public domain

Chapter 25
AvillaMO © Traveler7 CC BY-SA 3.0,

AvillaPostOffice © Eric Swanger, CC BY-SA 3.0
Chapter 26
Hotel Meade in Bannack Montana © Woolsterp, CC BY-SA 4.0
Bannack © Mr Hicks46, CC BY-SA 2.0
HenryPlummer, author unknown Public Domain
Chapter 27
HummelPark © Dj Romm13, CC BY-SA 4.0
MorphingStairs © Adam Fletcher Sasse, NorthOmahaHistory.com
Chapter 28
Luxor Hotel © Iconoteca dell'Accademia di architettura CC BY-SA 4.0
Luxor Hotel Lobby & Rooms © Rob Young CC BY 2.0
Chapter 29
BenjaminJamesHouse © Magicpiano, CC BY-SA 4.0
Chapter 30
NJDevil © Philadelphia Evening Bulletin, January 1909, Public Domain
Jersey-Devil © Various/several, Public domain
Chapter 31
Officers Quarters Fort Stanton © AllenS, Public domain
Fort Stanton - Unknown author, Public domain
Chapter 32
Mark Twain House © Ajay Suresh CC BY 2.0
Mark Twain © A.F. Bradley, Public domain
Chapter 33
Tar River © U.S. Department of Agriculture, Public domain
Banshee © W.H. Brooke, Public domain
Chapter 34
San Haven, North Dakota licensed under CC BY-SA 2.0
Public library, Bismarck, N. Dak ©Tichnor Bros.Inc, Public domain
Chapter 35
Moonville Tunnel © ChristopherM, CC BY-SA 3.0
Madison County Bridge © Historic American Buildings Survey (HABS), Public domain
Chapter 36
SatanicPurplechurch © Pull Over Adventures/Youtube
Chapter 37
Old Oregon Trail 1852-1906 © Ezra Meeker. Fourth Edition 1907, Public Domain
Ermatinger House - Oregon City © Ian Poellet, CC BY-SA 3.0
Chapter 38
Eastern State Penitentiary © Carol M. Highsmith, Public domain

Cellblock 4 © Adam Jones, Ph.D., CC BY-SA 3.0

Chapter 39

White Horse Tavern RI, originally uploaded by Swampyank at English Wikipedia., CC BY-SA 3.0

Ri-newport-jail-house © http://hauntedhouses.com

Chapter 40

Old Charleston Jail © Warren LeMay from Covington, KY, United States, CC0,

Chapter 41

Main street deadwood © Richie Diesterheft from Chicago, IL, USA, CC BY 2.0

Old Fairmont Hotel © Carol M. Highsmith, Public domain

Chapter 42

The death of John Bell, of Adams, TN. Occurred December of 1820. Illustration first published in 1894.

Chapter 43

Pine Uplands © William L. Farr, CC BY-SA 4.0

Chapter 44

Skinwalker Ranch © Paul from USA, CC BY-SA 2.0

Chapter 45

Bennington © King of Hearts, CC BY-SA 4.0

Somerset Reservoir © Jessamyn, Public domain

Chapter 46

Dr Ian Stevenson © 2007 by the Rector and Visitors of the University of Virginia

Chapter 47

Fort Worden © Mamabrooking, CC BY-SA 3.0

Fort Worden c.1923 © University of Washington, Public domain

Chapter 48

Abandoned Swings © Forsaken Fotos from Maryland, CC BY 2.0

Lake Shawnee Amusement Park © Forsaken Fotos from Maryland, CC BY 2.0

Chapter 49

Ghost Elephant © Derrick A. Mayoleth / Skillet Creek Media

Devil's Lake State Park, Wisconsin © http://www.goodfreephotos.com

Chapter 50

Old Bedlam - in Fort Laramie National Historic Site, Wyoming © Paul Hermans

Fort Laramie NHS-Gate © Chris Light at English Wikipedia, CC BY-SA 3.0

Licences

View links to creative commons licences used as indicated by the images attributed above at the below web addresses:

CC0 https://creativecommons.org/publicdomain/zero/1.0/
CC BY-SA 2.0 https://creativecommons.org/licenses/by-sa/2.0/
CC BY-SA 3.0 https://creativecommons.org/licenses/by-sa/3.0/
CC BY-SA 4.0 https://creativecommons.org/licenses/by-sa/4.0/

Permission has been granted for use of other images by their respective authors except in the case where the images appear in the public domain.

Printed in Great Britain
by Amazon